CW00701283

The Foragers'
Cookbook

countryside edition

James Wood

PROFESSIONAL FORAGER

The Foragers' Cookbook

Published by:
Totally Wild Publishing
www.totallywilduk.co.uk

Author James Wood

Designed by Kerry Slater

First Published in 2016, England

Copyright © Totally Wild Publishing

Publishers consent must be sought for reprint
(physical and digital) of any images and content.

All photographs are by and property of the author.

ISBN: 978-0-9956653-0-9 (Paper Back)
ISBN: 978-0-9956653-1-6 (E-book)
ISBN: 978-0-9956653-2-3 (PDF)

Disclaimer: At the time of printing the advice and
information within the contents of this book are
believed to be correct and accurate. Under no
circumstances can the author or publisher accept
any legal responsibility or liability for loss or
damage. This includes damage to property and/or
personal injury that may arise from any error or
omission from the information within this book.

Consumption of wild foods can potentially
cause allergic reaction in certain individuals.

With thanks to everyone who has helped
in the creation of this book.

The Forager's Cookbook

A Word From The Author

I am a professional, experimental, wild food forager based in the UK and I run in-depth, deeply engaging, wild food foraging and cookery experiences. This is done alongside sustainably collecting and processing a range of the most abundant wild edible plants for making preserves, which go to both local and regional restaurants and other establishments.

I've been amazed with the wild world from my childhood, finding great trees to climb, hills to roll down and even special twigs and stones to fill my pockets with. Over the past five years I've tested a vast amount of recipes, from making sweets from mushrooms, jam from flowers, coffee cake from roots and even down to making paper from mushrooms and glues from seaweeds. These tests have worked as an opportunity to establish, modify and finalise a range of tried and tested, successful recipes which are brought to you in an easy to follow guide throughout this book.

This book was created because I'm passionate about getting people to start interacting with their surrounding wild spaces. Hopefully it will give you the reassurance and confidence to do so through your taste buds. It is written in a way that will make foraging and cooking with wild foods more accessible.

Wild foods are linked to their most common commercially sold ingredient so you can start to use them as a substitute in any recipe that calls for these ingredients. For example nettles can be used as a substitute for cooked spinach. Each recipe gives you a wild ingredient, as well as easy to find store bought ingredients that you can substitute it for, should you not be confident enough to forage in the wild yet. This method allows you to add one wild ingredient at a time until you are confident enough to forage and harvest a larger range of wild ingredients.

Foraging from an uninformed perspective can seem difficult, but with a little of the right guidance, the art of foraging becomes easier over time and will lead to a greater understanding of the natural cycles of the year. Having the correct knowledge of your surrounding wild and overlooked green spaces allows you to collect free, healthy, fresh and local wild produce. I often grab my basket and head out to get my dinner from the park as anyone else might nip to the shops to buy theirs.

The Law & Foraging

When we're out foraging, there are a number of tips I always give people regarding sustainable foraging. The ways in which we can promote the growth of future plants and how we might interact with land owners for the benefit of everyone.

---

1. Never forage more that 40% of what's available. This is easy when it comes to trees as usually there are way more than 40% of leaves above what you can reach. However, with ground growing plants and small shrubs you can almost get lost in picking, and before you know it you've picked everything that's there.

2. Leave behind what you're not going to eat. If you are picking up stalks of a plant and need to discard the leaves before eating, then do this at the site where you've picked the plant. Leaving the leaves there will allow the nutrients to be absorbed back in to the ground making them available for future plants that grow here.

3. Never take the whole plant. If you take the top of the plant, i.e. stalks, flowers or leaves, then you must leave the roots. If you are harvesting the roots then you must leave the top parts of the plant – you have to show you're not depriving the land of the whole plant.

4. Get the land owners' permission to dig up roots. If you're digging the roots of a plant, there is a legal requirement to have the land owners' permission. I've found that if you offer to dig up people's dandelions for free then they will more than likely jump at the chance, as it saves them the time of doing it themselves and keeps their lawns fresh.

5. Be friendly and share your produce. Usually if I find a vast amount of a plant that I'd like to collect on someone's land, I would always ask the land owner before going and grabbing it. However, what I usually do is offer them some of the produce I'm going to make with it. For example, I collect elderflowers from a farmers field so I offer him a couple of bottles of elder flower cordial or sparkling wine. It's a win-win situation, and we're all aware of each other.

Bilberry

'vaccinium myrtillus'

Habitat:

Bilberries are found in woodlands, heaths and moors. They enjoy acidic soil and damp conditions.

Distribution:

Bilberry grows in the UK, Europe, Iceland to Spain, and Northern Asia,

Physical Characteristics:

Bilberries are a hairless low growing undershrub, covering large areas of land. They grow to a maximum height of 50cm, but can look taller when growing on sharply angled ground.

The flowers, appearing in clusters April-June, are globular or urn shaped, greenish turning pink with a length and width of 5-6mm.

The bright green leaves are oval shaped, often with a wavy margin and are finely toothed.

The purple to black fruit ripens from August through to September, growing within the whole shrub, making them more difficult to pick. They're globular shaped 5-6mm in length and width with an indented tip.

Medicinal Uses:

The leaves can be taken in tea for a prolonged period of time to aid diabetes as it reduces blood sugar levels. The berries are high in anthocyanins which can dilate blood vessels, helping lower blood pressure and have been recorded as promoting good eye sight.

Other Interesting Facts:

The people of Cheshire are said to eat the berries picked on Lammas with cream and milk for good luck.

The easiest way I've found to collect these berries is with a fruit picker, which also picks a lot of leaves with it. Then take the whole lot, place it on a table and blow over it with a hair dryer blowing cold – the leaves get blown away and the berries stay on the table.

Known Hazards:

The plant has a high tannin content and if eaten to excess can affect digestion. Avoid eating if taking anti-coagulating medication.

Could Be Confused With:

Bilberries could be confused with other closely related species in the Vaccinium Genus. Vaccinium uliginosum, vaccinium cespitosum, vaccinium deliciosum, vaccinium membranaceum, vaccinium ovalifolium all of which are similarly edible.

Edible Uses:

Leaves: green tea, fermented tea, dried tea, wine, smoking foods

Flower clusters: tea, syrup, salads, dessert decoration, candied

Berries: Jam, Jelly, tea, ice cream, sorbet, syrup, pies, pastries, muffins, cakes, fruit leather, wine

Bilberry & Apple Pie

I first began making this bilberry pie for my Grandma as it's one of her favourite foods. I've come to believe that the recipe below is the best for the pie as it makes your bilberries go quite far but also holds onto the fantastic flavours the bilberry has over its commercially grown cousin, the blueberry.

SERVES
8

Ingredients:

Pastry

- 300g plain flour
- 3 tbsp water
- 150g butter
- A pinch of salt

(alternatively you can use pre-made short crust pastry)

Filling

- 500g cooking apples, peeled and cored - cut these as you like, either diced or quartered
- 200g bilberries
- 25g butter
- 100g caster sugar

Method:

1. To make the pastry, add your flour, salt and butter to a large bowl and rub the mixture together until it resembles bread crumbs. Using your fingers is more fun but a spoon can be used.

2. Add the water, a teaspoon at a time, until your dough binds together sufficiently. Wrap this mixture in cling film and place in the fridge for 15 minutes.

3. To make the filling, heat the butter in a large pan and add the apples and sugar, leaving to cook for 5-10 minutes, depending on how soft you like your apples. Then add your bilberries and cook the lot for a further 2 minutes.

4. To bring the pie together, firstly you need to pre-heat your oven to 200C. Take a medium sized oven proof dish and rub more or any remaining butter all around the inside.

5. Roll out one half of your pastry and use this to line your dish. You can either flash bake this now or put your filling straight in.

6. Roll out the other half of your pastry and place it over your filling, on top of the dish and cut off any excess.

7. Using a knife cut two 3cm holes in the top of your pie, sprinkle with a little more sugar and leave to bake in the oven for 20 minutes.

8. Serve the pie hot with thick cream or lovely vanilla ice cream and enjoy.

Ingredients:

- 500g cooking apples, peeled & cored - cut them as you like, diced or quartered
- 200g bilberries
- 200g jam sugar

Method:

1. Put the apples in a large pan and cook on a medium heat for 10 minutes, until it starts to mush down slightly. Add the sugar and bilberries and cook for a further 5 minutes.

2. Put the whole lot in a blender and blitz until a smooth consistency is reached.

3. Boil this mixture until it starts to caramelise, usually around 30 minutes on a medium heat.

4. Once you've reached this stage, pour the mixture into two large non-stick dishes that are lined with baking parchment. Use at least 30x20cm tins. It's good to be spread thin so spread the mixture out over even more separate dishes if you have small ones – a thick spread in the tray will take forever to dry. Place in your oven on 100C. Leave the door of the oven slightly ajar and allow all of the liquid to evaporate from the mixture, I leave for 4 hours and then check how it feels. It should peel out of the tray easily and shouldn't feel wet or overly sticky. If it is, leave it in for another hour and try again. Depending on how much liquid was in the initial ingredients this can take up to 10 hours.

5. You should now be able to peel your fruit leather off your tray and can eat it straight away, or roll it up in the baking paper and store in an air tight jar. This is amazing preservation and should store for at least 1 year in your jar.

Bilberry &
Apple Fruit
Leather

Fruit leather always
reminds me of chewy
sweets and is the perfect
thing to take out on a
long walk as a snack.

Silver Birch
'betula pendula'

Habitat:

Silver Birch trees are usually found on open woodland and heath land. Found growing as a pioneer tree, they are the first to take over a site and they like an alkali soil.

Distribution:

Silver Birch is found growing throughout the UK, North America, Europe and Northern Asia

Physical Characteristics:

Silver Birch is a deciduous tree growing from 15-30m tall with a canopy of 5-10m. It tends to have a fairly slender trunk growing to a maximum diameter of 40cm. The bark on the trunk and branches begins golden brown turning a silvery white colour with age, which can often be seen peeling away from the tree. As it ages, the bark begins cracking and splitting open revealing a brown scar. The new shoots are thin and hairless, containing either male catkins at the tip or are shorter holding female catkins, which droop from the tree. These begin green, turning yellow and later brown when they drop their small, 1-2mm winged seeds in mass. The light green leaves, fading to yellow in autumn, have short stalks 3-5cm. They are triangular in shape with a broad base, double-toothed serrated margins and a slender pointed tip.

Could Be Confused With:

There are a huge range of Birch trees that have white, or whiting bark that rips from the base and bark of the tree, none of which are poisoness.

Medicinal Uses:

The bark of silver birch can be used as a diuretic and mild laxative. All parts of the silver birch can be used as a detoxifier and tonic for helping remove waste products from the urinary tract.

Known Hazards:

The tar present in the bark of this tree has been recorded as causing skin irritation. There's also reference of an insect that feeds on the sap of the silver birch leaves exuding a chemical called methyl salicylate which can cause irritation of the lungs.

Edible Uses:

Sap: edible, drunk as water, boiled to syrup, wine, cordial, toffee, ice cream, bbq glaze, sauce, sweetener

Leaves: edible when young, in salads

Young Catkins: edible

Bark: edible, ground into flour

Other Interesting Facts:

This tree can often be found growing in abundance in a single location. Somewhere that is a new space allowed to turn wild is a common spot to find it. There are a range of mushrooms that grow in association with this tree giving it other edible purposes and to help with identification of mushrooms.

To test that the sap is flowing in this tree, meaning it's ready to tap and extract the sweet sap, you can simply stab the sharp end of a knife through the bark and into the wood. If sap drips down your knife then it's ready for tapping (around the middle two weeks of March in the UK).

Birch Sap Syrup

Making Birch sap syrup is one of the first things I do with wild food every year. It tells me we're about to shoot straight into the more serious collection of wild foods and is, at the moment, my only source of wild sugar to be used throughout the coming year. The sap rises throughout March and can vary from year to year, but each area usually has a 2-3 week window to do this process. The easiest way to check if the sap is flowing is to stick a knife in the tree trunk at an upward angle, if sap leaks down the knife then you're good to go.

Equipment:

- Plastic tubing - 1cm in diameter and 40cm in length
- A drill - any will work, manual or electric
- 1cm drill bit
- Container for collecting sap - I use a 5 litre water bottle
- Piece of muslin cloth - big enough to cover the whole of the container
- A range of elastic bands or string

Method:

1. After checking whether the tree is flowing, about 1m up from the base of the tree, use your drill to make a 1cm wide hole, 8cm in to the tree. Push your piping into this hole, making sure it's at least 2cm in and secure.

2. Secure your container at the base of the tree – either tie it to the tree making sure it's on flat ground or secure it by leaning rocks against the sides.

3. Secure the cloth around the top of the container, either using elastic bands or string. Then pop a hole in the middle of your cloth and feed the tubing through it so the liquid will drip in to your container. Secure the cloth around your tubing with either string or an elastic band. This will ensure no insects can get into your container.

4. Leave it overnight to fill up then return to find your 5 litre container full of beautiful sap. Remove everything and pop the lid on your container so you can easily carry it away.

5. Take a branch, the same thickness as the original hole (1cm in diameter) and sharpen the end. Remove your tubing from the tree and hammer this branch bung in to the hole to bung up the tree.

6. Take your sap home and boil it down until it thickens and turns into a syrup. Up to 95% of the liquid must be boiled away so this can take a full day of boiling down. When it begins to thicken it needs constant stirring to ensure the sugars don't burn. Alternatively it can be put in a plastic bowl and in the microwave, opening the microwave door every minute to release the steam (I find it's less likely to burn this way).

7. When it has reached a consistency you're happy with, pour in to sterilised bottles or jars and enjoy.

Birch Sap Syrup BBQ Marinade

This marinade is perfect for the BBQ season or even for marinating and grilling food indoors when the weather takes a last minute turn for the worse! It's simple to make and will last in the fridge for up to 4 days. Meats that work well in this marinade are pork, beef and chicken. I try and marinade over night but a minimum of 1 hour will impart a lot of the great flavours. Once marinated, cook the meat as you would normally over the BBQ or Grill. This is a basic marinade...I urge you to explore and experiment with this basic recipe, adding additional spices that you enjoy. Use ginger and soy for a more oriental marinade or chilli powder and paprika for a spicy marinade...make it your own! This recipe will make enough marinade to coat 1 whole chicken.

Ingredients:

- 3 tbsp birch sap syrup

- 3 tbsp vegetable oil

- Juice of 1 orange

- 20g wild garlic finely chopped or 2 garlic cloves

- 4 fresh mugwort springs or thyme

- 1tsp finely ground alexanders seeds or black pepper

Method:

1. In a small pan mix all of the ingredients and simmer for 3 minutes until well combined.

2. Cool and store in the fridge or marinade the chicken straight away.

3. Marinade prior to cooking and brush on during cooking.

Birch Sap Jelly

This is a simple recipe that highlights the extraordinary flavour of the birch sap syrup. It requires no other flavouring and simply takes three ingredients. It can be made in advance and stored in the fridge, meaning it's simple for you to serve up...stress free!

Ingredients:

- 300ml water

- 3 tbsp birch sap syrup

- 3 leaves gelatine or a vegetable setting substitute

SERVES
4

Method:

1. Place the gelatine leaves in a bowl covered with cold water and allow them to soak for 5 minutes.

2. Bring 100ml of your water to a simmer and add the soaked gelatine leaves until they have fully dissolved. This should take about 3 minutes.

3. Add the rest of your water and birch sap syrup, stir until well incorporated.

4. Pour out into your serving vessels. I like to use thick bottomed glasses for this. Then leave the glasses in the fridge to set for 5 hours before serving.

5. Serve up with a good dollop of whipped cream.

Birch Sap Syrup Sticky Pudding

This soft, sticky pudding with textured sultanas and a birch syrup flavoured custard topping is my absolute favourite dessert. The flavours are deep, the pudding soft and the sauce soaks through the whole lot leaving us with a true celebration of birch sap syrup. This recipe will serve 6 people.

Ingredients:

Puddings

- 200g sultanas
- 1 tsp vanilla extract
- 2 eggs
- 1 tsp bicarbonate of soda
- 200g self raising flour
- 90g non salted butter, cubed
- 2 tbsp birch sap syrup
- 100ml full fat milk
- 150g brown sugar

Sauce

- 50g brown sugar
- 250ml double cream
- 6 tbsp birch sap syrup

Method:

1. Put the sultanas in a bowl and place in the microwave on high for 1 minute to soften them. Remove and stir in the vanilla extract.

2. In a large bowl, mix the flour and bicarbonate of soda. Then in a separate large bowl, beat the butter and sugar together. Add the eggs and birch sap syrup a little at a time and beat until it's all in.

3. To this mixture fold in the flour in a figure of eight. Use half of the flour and half of the milk to begin, adding it slowly until it's all combined, then pour in the sultanas. It may look like it's splitting a little but that's fine.

4. Spoon this mixture evenly between 6 small pudding tins about 200-250ml. Put in a pre-heated oven on 180C for 20 minutes.

5. Whilst the pudding is baking, put the sugar, butter and half the cream in a saucepan over a medium to low heat until all the butter has melted. Then stir in the birch sap syrup and allow the mixture to simmer for 3 minutes - stirring to make sure it doesn't burn. Remove from the heat and beat in the remaining cream.

6. Remove the puddings from the oven and leave to cool for 3 minutes. Using a palette knife or something similar, tease each of the puddings from their moulds onto your serving plates.

7. Pour over your warm sauce and enjoy. You could also leave the puddings in the fridge for 1 day to make them extra sticky, then microwave before eating.

Blackberry
'rubus fruticosus'

Habitat:

Blackberries or brambles are usually found on roadsides, verges, broadleaf woodland, hedgerows, gardens, canals, paths, railway sides, parks... almost everywhere.

Distribution:

A type or hybrid of blackberry can be found all over the world in places such as Australia, Asia, Europe, the UK, North and South America, China and Russia.

Physical Characteristics:

This scrambling shrub grows from 50cm-2m in length. The length of the plant's strong stem contains many thorns giving it its name "bramble". The stems new shoots start off in a star shape with a soft centre, turning more rounded and woody as they get older. The spear shaped leaves grow from 5-10cm, each containing 3-5 main teeth and being jagged along their whole edge. They are dark green on top and light green below.
The flowers are 2-3cm across, typically white to pink and contain 5 petals, flowering in bunches of up to 10.
This plant produces a large amount of fruit, which is why most people recognise this plant from picking it for making jam and pies.
It's certainly a childhood memory for me.

Known Hazards:

The stem of this plant contains many thorns and spikes, it's almost impossible to walk through brambles and it's fairly common to catch or even rip clothing when around brambles.

Other Interesting Facts:

f cut through winter they can be
e-thorned by running your hand
with fire gauntlets or a thick
cloth up the stem. They make
the most amazing weaving rods!
They're light and unbelievably
strong...it's almost impossible
to snap these rods. They're
extra-long and can be weaved
into almost anything; definitely
my favorite weaving material.
To use these for weaving it's
est first to dry the rods outside
for two weeks and re-hydrate
them in water for at least
12 hours before weaving.

Medicinal Uses:

The chemicals that are
responsible for the colour of
the blackberry are also mainly
responsible for most of the
healing benefits that are being
tested of blackberries. These
include flavonoids, salicylic
acid, polyphenols and other
phytochemicals, and are being
used in preliminary research
to aid the treatment of cancer.
Blackberries are high in vitamin
C, K and the nutrient magnese.

Edible Uses:

Root: Best collected in winter,
herbal use, could be incorporated
into a medicinal soup stock

Stem: Young spring growth,
candied, pickled, Can be used as
a vegetable in soup (boiling in a
number of changes in water)

Leaves: Edible when young
(good in pesto with wild garlic),
Traditional herbal tea

Fruit/seeds: Under ripe green
or red fruit can be pickled or
candied. Ripe fruit has numerous
uses from jam to juice, wine,
sauces, sorbet, cordial, syrup

Blossom: Tea infusion

Blackberry Jam

This jam recipe calls for the use
of less sugar and pectin than your
average recipe. The resulting jam is
more of a purée berry compote, but
it's great as the flavour of the berry
isn't overpowered or lost with the
heavy use of sugar.

Ingredients:

- 500g
  blackberries

- 200g caster
  sugar

- Juice of
  2 lemons

MAKES
2-3
MEDIUM
SIZED
JARS

Method:

1. Place the blackberries in
   a large pan and put it over
   medium heat for 10 minutes
   with the lid on.

2. After 10 minutes add
   the sugar and juice of 2
   lemons, then mash with a
   potato masher.

3. Continue cooking for a
   further 10 minutes, or
   until it's thick and juicy.

4. Remove from the heat
   and store in air tight,
   well cleaned jars.

5. Eat within 2 weeks and
   keep in the fridge.

Blackberry Stem Candy

Ingredients:

- 4 fresh blackberry shoots, with the spikes scraped off & finely chopped

- 40 bramble leaves

- 200ml boiling water

- 200g caster sugar

Method:

1. Place the bramble leaves and boiling water in a pan and boil for 15 minutes, with the lid of the pan on. Then pour through a sieve to remove the leaves.

2. To the liquid, add the sugar and stir until fully dissolved and remove from the heat. Then add the de-spiked and finely chopped bramble stems and leave to rest with the lid on for three days.

3. Remove the stems from the syrup and place on baking parchment, on a baking tray in the oven at 160C with the door open. Leave for 1-2 hours or until fully dry. You can boil the leftover syrup and store for future use.

4. They will be non-sticky and crunchy when ready. Store in an air tight jar and use in deserts and even salads to give a nice crunch

Blackberry Pickle

Ingredients:

- 4 fresh blackberry shoots with the spikes scraped off & finely chopped

- White wine vinegar

- 4 wild garlic bulbs or 2 garlic cloves

Method:

1. Add the de-spiked and finely chopped bramble stems and garlic to your jar and pour over the cold vinegar.

2. Leave for 3 weeks to pickle and then enjoy. Use within 1 year

MAKES
1
MEDIUM
JAR

Blackberry Stem Candy & Blackberry Pickle

This recipe was envisioned by a good friend of mine, Fergus Drennan. When thinking up new ways to interact with wild plants, it's difficult but very worthwhile to think through the potential of using different parts of the plants we commonly interact with. The stems of blackberries can be used when they're young between May and June; when they're new, vibrant green and still flexible. Even better, when they're chopped finely they give you an amazing star shape. So here's two quick recipes for using the stems of blackberries/brambles.

SERVES
2

Blackberry Sauce With Venison & Black Pudding

Blackberries were made for venison and venison for black pudding so it's a no brainer that the three of these should definitely be served up together. This meal is a good introduction to cooking with game meats.

Ingredients:

- 4 slices of good quality black pudding

- 100g blackberries

- 1 tbsp balsamic vinegar

- 2 thick venison steaks, well seasoned

- 100ml beef stock

- 100g butter

- 20g wild garlic stalks or 1 garlic clove

- 3 large potatoes, peeled & chopped

Method:

1. Boil the potatoes for 17 minutes, sieve and mash with 50g of the butter until nice and smooth, season well.

2. Heat the remaining butter in a pan and fry the venison and black pudding in this for 4 minutes on both sides.

3. Whilst this is frying, put the beef stock, balsamic vinegar and wild garlic in a pan with the blackberries and simmer for 4 minutes.

4. Remove the venison and black pudding from the frying pan and allow to rest for 1 minute.

5. Pour the left over juice from the frying pan in to your blackberry sauce and cook for a further minute.

6. Serve the venison on the mashed potato with the black pudding alongside it, and tenderly pour the blackberry sauce over the top.

Dandelion
'taraxacum officinale'

Habitat:

Dandelions grow everywhere and anywhere they can get their seeds to spread. This includes road sides, grassy banks, walls, cracks in paths, fields, hedgerows, gardens, waste lands and much more.

Distribution:

Dandelions are the most prolific of all weeds throughout the UK, and can also be found all over America, Canada and throughout Europe and Asia.

Physical Characteristics:

The Dandelion is an extremely effective perennial, having the ability to grow from seed and root segment. A single plant can produce up to 5,000 seeds, which have the ability to travel in the wind over 200 metres from their origin. They also do not need to be pollinated to reproduce. Dandelions grow above a sturdy taproot that can grow over 30cm down, forming a basal rosette of deeply lobed leaves.

The leaves can grow from 5-50cm long and 2-10cm wide. The leaves can vary slightly from one to another but all leaves are typically oblong or obovate in shape, becoming more narrow towards the base of the plant. The leaf edge ranges from being shallow to deeply lobed but they are always lobed in some way, giving them the appearance of lions' teeth.

A single flower head grows from a single, hollow leafless stem that can grow up to 50cm and on breaking exudes a white latex. The yellow flowers grow from a single centre and resemble an opened traditional Japanese umbrella. This umbrella eventually becomes a white puffball of seeds, which can easily be carried for dispersal by the wind.

Known Hazards:

Dandelion root tea is sometimes taken to increase people's appetite. What it also does is release sugar into the blood, so as a diabetic it is worth keeping this in mind if you're planning to drink Dandelion root tea. Those with very sensitive skin may get contact dermatitis when touching the latex, but it's also good for killing off warts!

Other Interesting Facts:

In order to decrease some of the bitterness sometimes present in the leaf, you can rip the two leaf edges away from the centre, removing the majority of the white liquid which causes the bitter taste. If you place a pot with a small hole in it over a young dandelion it will grow a large pale leaf which will be a lot less bitter, more tender, and delicate as a salad. Restaurants actually buy this stuff, it's like forcing rhubarb.

Could Be Confused With:

There are a range of other plants in the Asteraceae family known as false dandelions, in general plants in the Asteraceae family are considered safe, edible and herbal.

Dandelions also look very similar to Cat's Ears (hypochaeris radicata). The main differences being that Dandelion leaves are smooth or glabrous whereas Cat's Ears are coarsely hairy. The whole of a Cat's Ear plant is also edible, and the leaves are actually less bitter than those of the Dandelion.

Medicinal Uses:

Dandelion is mainly used as a liver tonic and diuretic. The white juice exuding from the stem is said to cure warts. Dandelion was historically known for treating a large array of ailments due to the large number of active compounds present within the whole plant.

Edible Uses:

Root: If collected late autumn, this can be roasted for coffee substitute or syrup. Tender roots are suitable for grating and lacto-fermenting, or roasted or boiled with Marmite (vegemite)

Stem: Use as a straw for drinking chilled dandelion flower tea, cordial or wine

Leaves: Fresh and early growth in spring can be used in salads, pasta dough, as a vegetable, for tisane, juicing, lacto-fermenting, pesto, a bitter for cocktails and beer making

Flower: For tea, cordial, salads, wine, marmalade, and tempura

Closed flower bud: (before going in to seed) as a vegetable

Fruit/seeds: For sprouting micro dandelions used in salads

Tips & Observations:

Dandelions that grow in the shade tend to have the largest and best edible leaves, whereas Dandelions growing in full sun produce the most amazing flowers. Just before picking the Dandelions, give the flower a sharp flick to knock away any potential bugs that may be resting in there.

Dandelion Root Roasted Coffee

Roasted Dandelion root doesn't have to be described as a coffee substitute as it has many of its own unique qualities which you just don't get from coffee. Firstly it's caffeine free, it doesn't have that acidic after taste you get from coffee and it also has this lovely velvety chocolate aroma that keeps me going back for more.

Preparing The Dandelion Roots:

1. Dig your dandelion roots. The best time for this is late September when they've grown larger. The easiest way to do so is to loosen the soil around the dandelion with a pitchfork before then digging out the root – if you don't there's a good chance the root will snap. Wash the roots removing any dirt and mud, then chop roughly into around 1cm cubes.

2. Place on a baking tray and put into a pre heated oven on 180C for 45 minutes. The key to doing this right is to leave the oven door open for the first 15 minutes.

3. Once out the oven, grind in a pestle and mortar or coffee grinder and store in an air tight jar.

Making The Coffee:

Ingredients:

- 1tsp Ground & roasted Dandelion roots per person

- 250 ml Boiling water per person

- Full fat milk to serve

- Birch sap syrup/honey to taste

Method:

Place your roasted Dandelion roots in a coffee plunger and top up with boiling water. Leave to infuse for around 8 minutes and then serve with full fat milk and birch sap syrup to taste.

Dandelion Bud Capers

When I'm out collecting dandelion flowers to make jam, I often find about 20% of the tops haven't opened up into flowers yet. So I decided to collect these as well and pickle them to use as a substitute to capers in recipes. It's incredibly simple...

Method:

1. When you have collected your Dandelion buds, place them in a jar along with a couple of garlic bulbs and cloves.

2. Pour over cold white wine vinegar and leave for 3 weeks before eating.

3. Use in any recipe that calls for capers. If they are heated, the flowers will open up so it's best to keep them cold and add them in at the end.

Dandelion 30 Leaf Salad

Realistically any mixture of wild edibles can be chucked into a bowl! When dressed with a tasty vinaigrette, something warm like wilted nettles or wild garlic and accompanied with something crunchy like croutons or fried bacon, it will taste just delightful. Some of the ingredients mentioned below haven't been discussed in detail in this book but can give you an idea of the types of salad you can create.

Ingredients:

- 50ml dandelion flower syrup
- 50ml apple cider vinegar
- A handful of croutons
- Any combination of the following leaves:

Cows Parsley, Hogweed Stem, Lesser Celandine, Common Daisy, Dandelion, Sow Thistle, Chickweed, Red Dead Nettle, White Dead Nettle, Yellow Dead Nettle, Nettle, Yarrow, Opposite Leaved Golden Saxifrage, Bramble, Wild Garlic, Bitter Cress, Hawthorn, Gorse, Darwins Barberry, Garlic Mustard, 3 Cornered Leek, Chive, Wild Lettuce, Water Mint, Ground Elder, Linden.

Method:

1. Loosely chop all of the leaves and place them in a large bowl.

2. In a pan place the dandelion flower syrup and apple cider vinegar. Heat until it simmers and pour over the leaves.

3. Adorn with the flowers and croutons and enjoy!

MAKES
3-4
MEDIUM
SIZED
JARS

Dandelion Flower Jam

This zesty and zingy marmalade has a flavour reminiscent of an apricot jam. It looks fabulous with dandelion petals suspended throughout and can be used straight on toast, scones or enjoyed in a more exotic manor by mixing with soy sauce and enjoying as a sweet dipping sauce.

Ingredients:

- 3 cooking apples - peeled, cored and chopped

- 50g fresh dandelion flowers or a good handful

- Juice of 3 lemons

- 750g jam sugar

- 600ml water

Method:

1. Put the peeled and cored apples in a pan with the hot water and 3/4 of the dandelion flowers (with green on). Simmer for 10 minutes until the apples are soft and the liquid is a vivid orange.

2. Strain the mixture through a sieve. Then add the strained liquid back to the pan and add the lemon juice and sugar.

3. Stir over a low heat until the sugar has dissolved and then add the rest of the dandelion flowers. Remove the green parts and use the petals only.

4. Boil the mixture vigorously until the setting point is reached. You can test this by putting a side plate in the fridge with a little jam on it. Remove the plate after 1 minute and if it has formed a skin, you will know that the setting point has been reached.

5. Place the mixture into steralised or well cleaned jars and leave to set. Store and use within 1 year. Once opened, keep in the fridge and use within a week.

Creamy Lamb With Dandelion Bud Capers

This is a true winter delicacy. The hearty and creamy mutton is cut through with our dandelion capers leading to a great taste combination.

Ingredients:

- Medium leg of lamb
- 100g butter, salted
- 200ml single cream
- 4tbsp dandelion top capers
- 3 onions, loosely chopped
- 3 diced carrots
- 4 peeled & chopped potatoes
- 1l beef stock
- 1 bottle white wine
- Sprig of rosemary & thyme

Method:

1. Place a cast iron dish or roasting tin over a hob and heat 25g butter. Add the lamb and cook until golden brown, turning every minute or so for around 4 minutes.

2. Add the beef stock, white wine, onions, potatoes, carrots, rosemary and thyme to the pan. Cover with the lid or tin foil and place in a preheated oven at 150C for 5 hours.

3. Remove the pan from the oven. Take out the lamb and wrap in tin foil to rest.

4. Whilst the lamb is resting, add the cream and butter to the vegetables along with salt and pepper to season.

5. Just before serving, chuck in the capers and pour over the rested lamb. Serve the pan straight on the table for everyone to dig straight in. A thick hearty bread goes great with this dish to soak up any leftover juices.

SERVES
5

Dandelion Root Coffee Cake

This cake is a classic for me. The roasted dandelion root imparts everything that's brilliant about it. It has a reminiscent flavour of chocolate without having to put any into the recipe. This can be made as a single or double tiered cake and should serve around 8 people.

Ingredients:

- 325g butter, softened
- 200g caster sugar
- 4 eggs
- 80ml root coffee
- 100g self raising flour
- 100g chestnut flour
  (if you can't find this you can use
  another 100g self raising flour)
- 200g icing sugar
- Hazelnuts for decoration

Method:

1. In a bowl beat 200g butter and 200g caster sugar until light.
   Then add 4 eggs; one at a time and mix thoroughly.

2. Add 50ml strong dandelion root coffee, 100g self-raising flour
   and 100g sweet chestnut flour and combine. It may look like
   it's curdling slightly but that's fine.

3. Spoon the mixture in to a well-greased cake tin and
   bake on 180C for 30 minutes.

4. Remove the cake from the oven and spray over the top
   some dandelion root extract or sprinkle a little more
   root coffee over the top.

5. Beat 125g butter with 200g icing sugar until light.
   Then add 30ml espresso and mix thoroughly.

6. Spread the mixture over the top of the cake and sprinkle
   crushed hazel nuts over. Enjoy with a cup of tea, in the
   afternoon with friends or after dinner.

Dandelion Flower Wine

This wine has been compared to tasting like the bliss of sunshine itself; it has a sweet, almost honey-like flavour that goes down so smoothly you need to keep a check on how much you've had.

Ingredients:

- 1 carrier bag of dandelion heads, around 250g

- 1.2kg white sugar

- 2 lemons

- 2 oranges

- 5 litres water

- 1 sachet yeast, bread or wine

- A demi-john or a 5l food grade container with hole and rubber bung in the top

- Air lock

It is key that all your equipment is thoroughly cleaned. This makes 5 litres at around 8% abv.

Method:

1. Pour a kettle full of boiling water over the dandelion tops and leave for 24 hours in a large pan with the lid on. If you don't have time, simply boil for 15 minutes instead.

2. Strain the dandelion tops from the juice and put the tops in compost. Keep the drained liquid.

3. To the remaining strained liquid, add the juice of the lemons and oranges, the sugar and remaining water and stir until all mixed in sufficiently. Add the yeast, put a cloth over the top of your pan and leave for 24 hours to start brewing/bubbling.

4. Pour this mixture into your demi-john and put on your airlock. Leave for as long as possible, at least 1 month.

5. Decant into your storage bottles and enjoy chilled on a sunny day. I always use plastic bottles just in case it continues to ferment and it becomes bubbly. The bottle will become tight and the gas can be released by un-screwing the lid slightly, like with fizzy drinks.

Elder

'sambucus nigra'

Habitat:

Elder enjoys moist and dry soils and is almost always found in a sunny spot. This tree can be found in hedgerows, woodlands, garden edges, farmers' fields, walkways, playing fields and commonly by canals.

Distribution:

The Elder tree is temperate to tropical regions of Europe, UK, Western Asia, North and Central America and Northern Africa.

Physical Characteristics:

Elder is a deciduous shrub or small tree, growing up to 6 metres tall and the same in width.

The bark of this tree is a light brown-grey and can be found cracking with a yellowing revealed in-between cracks.

The light green and lightly serrated leaves which are spear shaped, 5-12cm long and 3-5cm wide, grow in opposing pairs, arranged along a pinnate with five to seven pairs.

The flowers 5-6mm in diameter. Each have five petals and are borne in large, flat umbrellas which are 10-25cm in diameter.

The fruit grows similarly to the flowers in large collections. They are almost perfectly round, glossy dark purple and measure 5-6mm in diameter. They cause the branches they hang on to droop when they are ripe.

Known Hazards:

All green parts except the buds, flowers and fruit of this plant are considered poisons and should be avoided.

Could Be Confused With:

Elder can sometimes be confused with Ground Elder. This grows to a maximum of 1.5m high and among a huge array of differences does not have bark and is not a tree.

Rowan is another similar tree but the main difference is thet rowan leaves are heavily serrated.

Medicinal Uses:

The flowers are still used by herbalists now to aid inflammation within the respiratory system, including asthma, coughs and hayfever. The berries are commonly used and stored within syrups, jams, wines and juices to give a boost of vitamins and minerals throughout the winter months, helping to ward off the common winter ailments.

Other Interesting Facts:

If you cut a branch from this tree, the inside or pith can be pushed out fairly easily using a tent peg or another hard piece of wood. This hollow wood can now be used for loads of things. For example, making jewellery, beads, pennies, snakes, whistles and even blow darts.

Edible Uses:

Leaves: Herbal use as a strong anti-viral (can cause nausea and vomiting)

Immature flower buds: Pickling, Lacto fermenting

Flowers: Cordial, Sparkling Wine, Tempura, Tea, Ointments

Fruit: Best heated, Wine, Syrups, Juice, Fruit Leather, Cordial, Beers, Ketchup, Chutney, Jam, Frozen in Desserts

Elderflower Cordial

I advise everyone to make some elderflower cordial! It's the perfect way to preserve the delicate flavours we get from the elder. Once you have the cordial you can then use it to add this flavour to loads of things; from cheese cakes to sorbets, ice lollies, cocktails, cupcakes, flavoured icing and even elderflower prosecco.

Ingredients:

- 500g caster sugar

- Juice of 3 lemons

- 10 elder flower heads

- 750ml water

MAKES 1 LITRE

Method:

1. Heat the water and dissolve the sugar in it. Add the rest of the ingredients and simmer for 10-20 minutes.

2. Strain off the liquid through a cloth or fine sieve and pour into sterilised or cleaned bottles.

3. Store in the fridge and use within 2 months.

4. This drink is served nicely with ice and still or sparkling water. It's also nice to pour the cordial in to ice cube trays to easily add an elderflower ice twist to drinks.

Ingredients:

- 2kg elder berries
- 3.5l water
- 1.1kg caster sugar
- Juice of 1 lemon
- Juice of 2 oranges
- 1 sachet of wine yeast or 13g bread yeast

MAKES
5 LITRES

Method:

1. Add the elderberries and 2 litres of water to a pan and bring to the boil with the lid on. After 10 minutes, using a potato masher, give the berries a good mashing until all the juice is extracted.

2. Let this cool for an hour then strain it through a muslin cloth. Bring the edges of the cloth into the middle, tie a knot and use your hand to squeeze as much juice from the berries as possible. You will use the extracted liquid but be sure to save the berries too but keep them separate.

3. To this liquid add the remaining 1.5 litres of cold water, the juice of the lemons & oranges and the sugar – stir until the sugar is dissolved. Sprinkle your yeast over the top and stir again.

4. Pour into a demi-john and secure an airlock in the top. Let this ferment for a minimum of 2 weeks; ideally up to 1 year.

5. Pour into sterilised bottles and enjoy! However, I allow my elderberry wine to age for a further year before drinking. This is the point where you could add 500ml brandy and 100ml elderberry syrup if you want to make it in to a port. If you saved the initial squeezed berries – you can follow the same procedure to make more of a rosé style wine, using the left over berry pulp. Lighter in flavour and more delicate.

Elderberry Wine

Elderberries contain a huge amount of flavour notes. They also contain suitable amounts of tannin to make them especially good when turned into a deliciously deep, earthy and fruity red wine. Furthermore, with the addition of brandy and elderberry syrup this makes and amazing elderberry port. This wine is best served with game meats or as a night time tipple.

Elderflower Sparkling Wine

This is by far my favourite sparkling version of a wild wine you can make! I currently make 25 litres of this stuff every year, and it barely lasts half of the year before it's all been drunk. It goes down well at every occasion from a dinner party to an afternoon BBQ and even goes down well on our pop up wine tasting evenings. It's incredibly simple to make and the key is that less is more with the flower heads – don't get carried away and put more in thinking it will give more flavour – it doesn't need it.

Ingredients:

- 1.1kg caster sugar

- 5 elder flower heads

- 2 lemons

- 2 oranges

- 1 sachet of yeast, either bread or wine

- 4.5l water

- Demi-john & air-lock

Method:

1. Chop your lemons and oranges into quarters and squeeze their juice into a pan. Throw the rest of the used lemons and oranges in the pan as well. Then add your elderflowers and 2 litres of the water.

2. Bring to the boil for 10 minutes with the lid on the pan. Then remove from the heat and strain through a muslin cloth, saving the liquid.

3. To this hot liquid add the sugar and stir vigorously until it is all dissolved. Then add the rest of the cold water.

4. Pour the yeast in, stir and pour into your demi-john. Pop the air-lock on and leave for 10 days to bubble away.

5. Siphon off into plastic bottles and for every 250ml add 1 teaspoon white sugar. Leave for another 5 days to carbonate and enjoy! Check the bottles every so often to make sure there isn't too much pressure inside. Plastic bottles will expand a little letting you know how much pressure is inside. If they feel too solid, slowly open the lid to release some pressure and then close again.

MAKES
5 LITRES

Elderberry & Apple Beef Stew

This winter stew utilises the earthy and wholesome
flavours of elderberries and the tart sweetness
of Bramley apples to create a true winter masterpiece.
Even better – if you don't eat all of it at once, you
can use the left overs to make an elderberry,
apple and beef pie for the next day.

Ingredients:

- 3 onions, peeled & roughly chopped
- 500g carrots, roughly chopped
- 600ml beef stock
- 800g stewing beef, cubed
- 3 garlic bulbs
- 300ml elderberry wine, blackberry wine or other red wine
- 12 whole elderberry heads
- 6 medium bramley apples, cored

Method:

1. In a large bottomed, oven safe dish or baking tray, heat some oil on the hob and brown the beef cubes all over for 3-4 minutes.

2. Add the carrots and onions and cook for a further 3 minutes. Next, add the garlic, beef stock and wine and put the lid over your dish or tightly secure tinfoil over the top.

3. Place in a pre-heated oven at 160C and leave to cook for 2 hours. After this time, remove from the oven and put in the cored apples and whole elderberry heads. Make sure the apples are fully submerged.

4. Place back in the oven for a further 8 minutes, or until the apples have softened.

5. Serve up so that everyone gets one apple and two elderberry heads. Enjoy with thick cut bread to soak up excess juices and some oven or fresh chips.

Elderflower Cheesecake

This cheesecake recipe will give you a beautifully light, creamy and irresistible dessert to wow your family with at the end of a Sunday roast, or surprise guests with at a Saturday night dinner party. The cheesecake topping melts in your mouth, giving you the delicate flavours of elderflower, while the crunchy base gives an exciting contrast.

Ingredients:

- 170g digestive biscuits

- 50g unsalted butter

- 500g full fat soft cheese

- 300ml whipping cream

- 3 tbsp elderflower cordial

- 2 tbsp icing sugar

SERVES
12

Method:

1. To make the cheesecake base, melt the butter and crush the digestives, then thoroughly mix the two together. Put this mixture in the base of a cake tin and use the back of a spoon to push it down, ensuring it's firm and even. Place this in the fridge to cool whilst we make the topping.

2. In a bowl mix the soft cheese with the elderflower cordial and icing sugar until smooth and even. In a separate bowl whip the cream until it's light and fluffy.

3. Fold the soft cheese mixture into the cream and spoon over the set crumble base.

4. Chill in the fridge for three hours, then enjoy with cream and a cup of roasted dandelion root coffee.

Hawthorn
'crataegus monogyna'

Habitat:

Hawthorn is native to the UK and has a historical use in hedge rows around farmers' fields, although this is less common in Scotland. It will grow on acid and most other soils, heaths, rocky and open areas. It can be found in scrubs, thickets, woodland and open areas although we mainly find it growing on moist soil.

Distribution:

Hawthorn grows well in northern Europe and over the majority of America but mainly in the north and also Asia.

Physical Characteristics:

This large shrub or small tree can grow from 5-14m tall and grows an extremely dense crown. Its bark ranges from mid-dark brown and typically contains upward running orange cracks. The tree itself tends to grow twisted and contorted, making it look mythical, and the young branches contain many thorns.

Hawthorn leaves are dark green on top and light green underneath, they can grow from 2-5cms in length, are obvate or teardrop shaped and deeply lobed.

The flowers, which are produced around May, have both female and male reproducing parts. They can be found in corymbs of 10-25 together. Each flower is about 1cm in diameter and contains 5 white petals and are slightly fragrant.

In autumn where there once stood flowers you will now find haws, the trees fruit that resembles a 1cm round red berry, although it is actually the structure of a pomme, containing a single seed.

Could Be Confused With:

This Hawthorn could quite easily be confused with the Blackthorn (Prunus Spinosa) or the Sloe bearing tree which does look quite similar. The easiest way to differentiate between these two plants is in spring; as the Hawthorn goes into leaf before flower, the Blackthorn will go into flower before leaf.

Known Hazards:

As its name implies, Hawthorn contains many thorns up its branches which can give a good prick. If you're on blood thinning medication it is not advised to eat lots of this plant, consult your doctor for this.

Medicinal Uses:

Linking to the folklore of Hawthorn being an extremely protective plant, it is used in herbal medicine to help heart ailments. The chemical proanthocyanidin found within the leaves, flowers and fruit of Hawthorn can lower blood pressure.

Other Interesting Facts:

Hawthorn wood is an extremely hard wood and works really well for carving, turning and working with. It gives a pale finish and cuts very well. If you have enough time and patience you can tap and collect the sap from the Hawthorn during spring, as you would with Pine. This can then be used instead of Gum Arabic in the production of wild watercolours, although it shrinks a lot more than Gum Arabic when drying, and this should be kept in mind.

Edible Uses:

Leaves: Edible when fresh and young, in salads and pasta dishes

Flowers: Edible, in teas, syrups, cakes

Fruit: Edible and can be made into ketchup, chutney, fruit leather and tomato pureé

Hawthorn Berry Chutney

This deep chutney is perfect with cheese and biscuits, giving a smooth sweet and sour flavour expected from any good chutney. It also goes well in cheese sandwiches as well as in a classic chilli.

Ingredients:

- 8 red onions peeled & chopped

- 200g brown sugar

- 150ml balsamic vinegar

- 150ml red wine vinegar

- 200g hawthorn berries

Method:

1. Remove any stalks and green bits from the hawthorn berries, add them to a large pan with 150ml red wine vinegar and let them boil for 15 minutes, with a lid on the pan.

2. Once boiled, remove from the heat and give the mixture a good mash with a potato masher. Strain this mixture through a sieve to remove stones and seeds, keep the pulp mixture that has passed through.

3. Put the chopped onions in a frying pan and fry off with 100g brown sugar until golden brown and softened for around 5 minutes.

4. Add your berry juice, fried and caramelised onions, the rest of the brown sugar and balsamic vinegar to a large pan and boil together for 5 minutes. Boil for longer if you prefer a thicker chutney.

5. Place in a well cleaned jar and then enjoy with a strong cheese.

MAKES 3-4 MEDIUM SIZED JARS

Hawthorn Berry Fruit Leather

This fruit leather is really wholesome and, although in this recipe I've added some apple, you could actually do this with solely hawthorn berries. They're fairly easy to collect and can be made into this fruit leather with little effort, even if it seems like a long time.

MAKES
30
PIECES

Ingredients:

- 300g cooking apples, peeled, cored and finely chopped
- 300g hawthorn berries
- 100ml water
- 200g jam sugar

Method:

1. Add the water and whole hawthorn berries to a pan and boil for 15 minutes with a lid on.

2. Using a potato masher, mash the hawthorn berries well in the pan. Then pass this mixture through a sieve to remove the stones and extract a thick pulp like mixture.

3. Add the cooking apples to a pan and cook for 10 minutes until softened. Then add the hawthorn berry pulp mixture, sugar and heat until the sugar has dissolved. Once dissolved, add the mixture to a blender and blend until smooth.

4. Add back to the pan and heat until it begins to thicken and caramelise (around 30 minutes) – if you're worried about this burning it can also be done in a microwave, 1 minute on high and then open the door and let the steam escape. Repeat this around 10 times until the mixture is super thick.

5. Once you've reached this stage, pour the mixture into two large non-stick dishes with a lining of baking paper and place in your oven on 100C/200F/Gas mark 3. Use at least 30x20cms. It's good to be spread thin so separate the mixture into even more dishes if you have small ones – a thick spread in the tray will take forever to dry. Leave the door of the oven slightly ajar and allow all of the liquid to evaporate from the mixture. I leave for 4 hours and then check how it feels – it should peel out of the tray easily and shouldn't feel wet or overly sticky. If it is I leave it in another hour and try again (depending on how much liquid was in the initial ingredients this can take up to 10 hours).

6. You should now be able to peel the fruit leather off the tray & eat it straight away, or roll it up in the baking paper & store in the fridge or air tight jar. This is amazing preservation and should store for at least 1 year in your jar.

Hawthorn Flower Tea

Hawthorn flower tea is not only a beautiful hot drink, it also has numerous health benefits. It's been used for strengthening the heart, increasing blood flow and reducing blood pressure.

Ingredients:

- A handful of fresh hawthorn flowers

- 1 litre boiling water

Method:

1. Put your fresh flowers in a tea pot or split amongst 4 cups

2. Pour the boiling water over the hawthorn flowers and put the lid on your pot, or cover the top of your cup with a side plate or something suitable.

3. Leave to infuse for 10 minutes

4. Enjoy this lovely flavour in the knowledge that your taste buds and heart will be happy for it.

MAKES
4 CUPS

Hazel

'corylus avellana'

Habitat:

Hazel is found growing on calcareous soils often in hedgerows and woodlands where it is used for hedging or coppicing.

Distribution:

Hazel grows in the UK, Europe, Norway, North and West Asia. Similar Hazel is found in North America.

Physical Characteristics:

The common Hazel is typically found as a shrub reaching 2-8m tall where it's coppiced. However when it's left to grow un-coppiced it can reach 15m tall. The bark is grey brown, becoming darker with age and eventually slightly peeling away. The fresh young shoots are hairy.

The leaves, 6-12cm long and across, are rounded with a double serrated margin and hairs on both sides.

The flowers are formed in early spring before the leaves. The catkins come in two forms, male and female. Male, 5-12cm long, are pale yellow whilst the female are 1-3mm long, bright red, and are mostly concealed in the buds.

The 15-20mm spherical, yellow-brown nut comes in a short leafed husk. They form in clusters of 1-5 together and will fall to the ground when they are ripe between September - October.

Other Interesting Facts:

You have to get out early to collect these nuts before the squirrels get them! Find a spot where you know they are and return weekly when you expect hem to come into season around early September. Alternatively, hey can be picked straight from the tree and used fresh. They are one of the few nuts that taste brilliant straight off the tree like this.

Although we only have one recipe in this book including Hazel, I have included it above all other nut producing trees as it produces the one wild nut I pick on a regular basis... when :hey're green and I can beat the quirrels to them! I then use this nut in any recipe that calls for either fresh or crushed nuts of any kind.

In folklore, Hazel has a strong link with poets, literature and gaining wisdom.

Medicinal Uses:

The oil of Hazel is referenced as being used to treat infection of threadworm or pinworm in young children.

Could Be Confused With:

Hazel could be confused with other species in the Corylus family, of which are similarly used. Linden Tree (Tilia) has a similar leaf structure but grows to a huge size, doesn't produce hazel nuts and isn't poisoness.

Edible Uses:

Leaves: green tea, fermented tea, dried tea, wine, smoking foods

Catkin: edible

Green nut: salads, pasta, feta parcels, milk

Ripe Nut: salads, pasta, cakes, pesto, flour, roasted, pickled, salted, soups, milk, oil

Hazel Nut Praline

Hazel nuts can be utilised in a multitude of recipes, I've included them in this guide as I use hazel nuts in any recipe that calls for nuts or mixed nuts... crushed in pesto, on top of cakes and much more. Hazelnut praline is a cracking accompaniment to any dessert, giving the dish a little crunch that it may have previously been missing. This recipe makes one slab which will serve around 10 desserts.

Ingredients:

- 70g caster sugar

- 70g hazelnuts

- 1tsp lemon juice

Method:

1. Place the sugar and lemon juice in a saucepan and heat over a medium heat until it's melted down into a liquid.

2. Add the hazelnuts and stir to coat them all over with the mixture.

3. Pour the mixture out on to a piece of baking paper and leave to cool for 30 minutes.

4. Smash up the slab and serve with whatever you like... on top of cheesecake, with yoghurts, ice cream, pies, jellies or just eat as it is for a little mid forage snack.

Hogweed

'heracleum sphondylium'

Habitat:

Hogweed prefers nitrogen rich soils and grows well up to an altitude of 2500m. It can be found on roadsides, banks, hedgerows, boarders, disused and waste land.

Distribution:

These plants grow all over Europe (except Iceland), North Africa and all over America and Asia.

Physical Characteristics:

Hogweed is a herbaceous perennial or biennial plant that can grow from 50-120cm in height. The main stem rises from a large reddish rhizomatous root. It is striated or ribbed, hollow and has bristly hairs all over.

The leaves can reach a length of 55cm. They are very pinnate, hairy and serrated, and are divided in to 3-5 lobed sections. The edges are typically round, unlike giant hogweed which are always extremely pointed. Hogweed has white to pinkish flowers, displaying in large umbels (umbrella looking) up to 25cm. Each contains 15-30 individual flowers and these individual flowers contain 5 petals. The seeds are winged and flattened, contained in pods with rounded edges and up to 1cm long.

Known Hazards:

A mild case of photo-phyto-dermatitis can be caused by touching the raw juice of this plant, and leaving the exposed skin in the sun will cause the area to blister. Wear gloves if picking and if the juice goes on you, keep that area of skin covered and out of direct sun light.

Could Be Confused With:

Hogweed is likely to be confused with Giant Hogweed but this is a lot larger. The leaves are a lot more sharp and you can typically see the remnants of last years growth from the huge canes (6-10ft) that will be left over.

Medicinal Uses:

It's referenced that the seeds have been used medicinally in the past, being heated in oil and applied to the skin for shingles. Also a decoction of the seeds was to be used for aiding a running ear.

Edible Uses:

Root: edible, grated, lacto fermented, alcohol infusions

Stem: steamed, chopped in salads, battered, fried, on pizzas and omelettes

Leaves: soups, dried as seasoning

Fruit/seeds: as cardamom in cakes, cookies, shortbread, chutney, rice, curries, as celery salt, infused alcohol

Other Interesting Facts:

When all of the smaller leaves have grown, you often get new shoots appearing half way up previously growing shafts. They can be found either in or emerging from paper looking sheaths. These can be used exactly the same as the really young shoots.

Personally I never wear gloves when picking this plant. Of course I don't purposefully rub the juice on myself, but I've never had an issue with the juice. If you plan to collect a lot of hogweed or even a little, wearing gloves, maybe marigolds, would be a safe bet, but don't worry yourself too much!

Tempura Battered Hogweed Stems

This is a simple and quick way to utilise hogweed stems with ingredients we all most likely have lying around in our cupboards. The batter gives a strong crispy outer edge to the succulent hogweed stems without destroying any of the refreshing flavour.

Ingredients:

- 15 young hogweed stems

- 50g cornflour

- 80g plain flour

- 1 tsp baking powder

- 250ml soda water

Method:

1. In a large bowl mix the baking powder, corn flour and plain flour together. Make a well in the centre and slowly add the soda water, stirring in between pouring, until it's all added and you have a smooth batter.

2. Bring some oil up to medium heat in a non-stick pan.

3. Dip the hogweed stems in the batter and fry on both sides until golden brown – about 2-3 minutes on each side.

4. Lightly salt and serve with a nice dip - hummus or wild garlic mayonnaise go nicely.

Steamed Hogweed Stems

This is the simplest, most delicate and enjoyable way to eat hogweed stems. It makes a great side dish and can accompany a vast array of meals from fish through to chicken.

Ingredients:

- 10 hogweed stems
- 50ml boiling water
- 50g salted butter

SERVES
2

Method:

1. Place the hogweed stems in a large pan with the boiling water. Bring to the boil and leave the lid on the pan for 3 minutes.

2. Add the butter and steam for another minute.

3. Remove the stems, and boil the liquid down, reducing it by half, and pour over the stems.

4. Season with salt and pepper and enjoy this spring delicacy.

Hogweed Rice Pancakes With Cob Nut Hoisin Sauce

This dish was inspired by food eaten during a visit to Vietnam. The rice pancake is truly incredible and I had to make a wild version of it to serve on cookery classes, so here it is for you to enjoy!

SERVES
3

Ingredients:

Pancakes

- 1 cup rice flour
- 1 tsp turmeric powder
- 230ml water
- 50g cubed & fried bacon
- 6 dandelion leaves or other salad leaves
- 6 water mint leaves or other mint
- 3 wild garlic leaves or 1 garlic clove

Dipping Sauce

- 1 tbsp hazlenut butter
- 2 tsp soy sauce
- 1 tsp fish sauce
- 1/2 tsp birch sap syrup or caster sugar
- 1 tsp seasame oil
- 20g wild garlic, finely chopped or 2 garlic cloves

Method:

1. To make the hoisin dipping sauce, add all the ingredients to a saucepan and bring to a simmer for 2 minutes until they are all well combined.

2. In a bowl mix together the rice flour and turmeric, then add the water, mix thoroughly and leave to rest for 15 minutes. If you can't find rice flour, place 1 cup regular rice with 1 cup water in a blender and leave to soak overnight. The next day blend the mixture together and pour through a fine sieve.

3. Heat a little oil in a small non-stick frying pan and then, like making ordinary pancakes, ladle in your rice pancake mixture.

4. Cook for 1-2 minutes on this side then flip and cook for a further 1-2 minutes on the other until nicely golden brown on both sides.

5. In the middle of the pancakes, add a little bacon, 2 dandelion leaves, 2 water mint leaves and a wild garlic leaf. Fold up the pancakes and enjoy with the hoisin dipping sauce!

Hogweed Stem & Chorizo Egg Tart

This simple dish can be cooked up and eaten hot or cold, meaning you can make it whenever you get time. Enjoy it as a whole meal with salad or sweet potato chips.

Ingredients:

- 3 large free range eggs

- 100ml single cream

- 6 ready made small tart crusts

- 100g chorizo

- 12 young hogweed stems

- A pinch of grated mature cheddar for each tart

Method:

1. In a jug mix your eggs and cream thoroughly and season with salt and pepper.

2. Pour your mixture into your tart crusts

3. Slice your chorizo and add to your tarts evenly.

4. Put 2 hogweed stems in each tart and sprinkle some cheese over the top.

5. Place in a preheated oven at 200C for 15 minutes.

6. Remove and enjoy with chickweed or other salad.

Hogweed Seed Spring Chicken Tray Bake

The chicken and hogweed tray bake has a fresh, vibrant and slightly floral flavour which sits perfectly on those warm summer evenings. It's quick to make and can be prepared the day before and chucked in the oven when you're feeling hungry. You could even prepare a couple and freeze them ready to be cooked after defrosting.

SERVES
4

Ingredients:

Chicken

- 6 chicken thighs
- 150ml chicken stock
- 1 tsp ground hogweed seeds or 1/2 tsp cardamom
- 3 cornered leek stems or 1 leek
- 16 young hogweed shoots or asparagus
- 100g sugar snaps
- Juice of 1 lemon

Potato Salad

- Handful of chopped cows parsley or normal parsley
- 800g new potatoes
- 3 tbsp mayonnaise
- 1 tbsp dandelion top capers or normal capers

Method:

1. Put your new potatoes in a pan with salted boiling water and boil for 20 minutes. Strain, add the cow's parsley, mayonnaise and dandelion capers then lightly mix.

2. Lightly fry the skin side of the chicken in a hot frying pan for 5 minutes until golden.

3. Put all of the vegetables in an oven dish and place the chicken thighs on top. Pour over the chicken stock and then sprinkle the thighs with some delicious ground hogweed seed seasoning.

4. Put this in a preheated oven at 200C for 35 minutes until the chicken is cooked through.

5. Remove from the oven and squeeze over the juice of one lemon. Serve up with your wild herby potatoes and enjoy!

Hogweed Seed & Cinnamon Shortbread Cookies

Hogweed isn't only limited to savoury dishes, this recipe calls for the hogweed seeds to take on sweet flavours and it does so perfectly, acting as a cardamom substitute.

Ingredients:

- 200g plain flour

- 200g unsalted butter

- 80g caster sugar

- 2 tsp ground hogweed seeds, crushed & sieved

- 1 tsp ground cinnamon

SERVES 10

Method:

1. In a large bowl place the flour, sugar, hogweed seeds and cinnamon, mixing them together well.

2. Cut the butter into small cubes and mix in thoroughly with the other ingredients.

3. Form the mixture into a ball, wrap in cling film and leave to rest in the fridge for 1 hour.

4. Place some baking paper on a baking tray, remove the mix from the fridge and split into as many cookies as you'd like, dependent on the size of cookie. I usually make 10 from this mix.

5. Place your cookies on the baking paper and put in a pre-heated oven on 180C for 10-15 minutes or until golden on top.

6. Remove from the oven and leave 10 minutes to cool. Enjoy them straight away or within 1 week.

Japanese Knotweed

'fallopia japonica'

Habitat:

Japanese Knotweed is typically found on roadsides, railway banks, rivers, 'waste'-ground, and similar areas, especially in urban and suburban landscapes.

Distribution:

Japanese Knotweed is found throughout the entire UK and mainland Europe, from Northern Italy to Norway.

Physical Characteristics:

Japanese Knotweed is a hardy, herbaceous, rhizomatous perennial. Plants are fully dioecious, with all individuals of the UK clone being functionally female. Rhizomes measure up to 10cm in diameter, bearing nodes at 1-2cm spacings, and extend generally up to 7 metres from the parent plant (though distances of 20 metres have been recorded). The rhizome penetrates downward to a depth of 2 metres or more. Stems can reach 3 metres high and are stout, hollow and bamboo-like with erect bases that eventually branch. Stems are sometimes red-brown, but often green and are smooth, with thinly membranous sheath. Leaves are wide at the base with the tips abruptly tapering to a point. The leaves measure 5-12cm wide and 5-15cm long, petioles 1-3cm long and stipules 8-15mm long. The female flower is greenish-white and drooping. Flowers are 2.5-3mm across in dense, branched, auxiliary panicles, which are 5-9cm long.

Could Be Confused With:

Japanese Knotweed could be confused with Giant Knotweed (Fallopia sachalinensis), or hybrids between the two species. However these are all similarly edible too.

Known Hazards:

Oxalic acid and oxalates are mild nephrotoxic acids that are abundantly present in the stem and leaves of Japanese Knotweed. This also the case with such plants as fat hen, rhubarb and sorrel. They won't cause an issue in regular amounts, but could cause a problem if eaten on mass.

Medicinal Uses:

The roots of Japanese Knotweed are used to help treat Lymes Disease.

Other Interesting Facts:

To ensure you pick only the tender stems, gently bend back the stem from the top of the plant. Like asparagus, it should snap at the tender point leaving you with a piece between 2-20cm long. Finally, it should be noted that it is illegal to cause the spread of this plant. Therefore all off-cuts should be burnt, boiled or allowed to rot before composting, not thrown in the bin.

Edible Uses:

Root (Sept- March): Starch can be extracted (with caution) and used as a thickener like cornflour

Stem - April/May: Young tender stem tops can be eaten raw or cooked and used as a rhubarb substitute for crumbles, pies, sorbets, sauces, pickling, and in both sweet and savoury dishes

Flower Buds (May-Aug): Can be used for wine, beer, and tisane making

Japanese Knotweed & Ginger Jam

This is a retake on the classic rhubarb and ginger jam, and as expected the flavour combination is absolutely perfect.

Ingredients:

- 800g young knotweed stems chopped in to 1cm pieces
- 1kg jam sugar
- 1 lemon, juice and zest
- 1 thumb sized piece of ginger, skinned and finely chopped

Method:

1. Place all the ingredients in a large bowl, mix thoroughly and allow to sit, covered, for 1 hour.

2. Next, place the mixture in a large pan over medium heat for 10-15 minutes, until the knotweed has softened.

3. Turn the heat up to high and let it boil vigorously until the setting point has been reached. To test this, put a small plate in the fridge and drop a tea spoon of boiling jam on to it. Put it back in the fridge for 30 seconds then remove it and push the jam with your finger. If the top wrinkles it's at setting point. If not continue cooking and testing until it works.

4. Pour your jam in to sterilised jars, seal and label - use within 6 months and 1 week after opening.

MAKES
3-4
MEDIUM
SIZED
JARS

Japanese Knotweed Curd

This Japanese Knotweed curd is smooth and velvety. It's absolutely perfect and best suited served with afternoon tea on scones. Once made it must be stored in the fridge and used with one week, but I can guarantee it won't last any longer than that...it tastes so good!

MAKES
3-4
MEDIUM
SIZED
JARS

Ingredients:

- 500g young knotweed stems, chopped
- 100ml water
- 4 large eggs
- 200g butter
- 150g caster sugar
- 1 tbsp cornflour

Method:

1. Put the knotweed stems in a pan with the water and place on the heat for 15 minutes, until the knotweed is fully softened and falling apart.

2. Pass the knotweed juice through a muslin cloth or fine sieve. Push lightly to remove the juice but not too much otherwise your juice will end up green instead of pink. Leave to cool for 30 minutes.

3. Add all your ingredients and 250ml of the knotweed juice to a pan that is set over a very low heat. Mix thoroughly until all of the butter has melted. Leave the pan on a low heat and stir continuously for 10 minutes or until your mixture has reached the consistency of custard.

4. Once you have acheived this consistency, sieve this mixture into a clean bowl to remove any egg that may have scrambled.

5. Pour into clean, sterile jars then keep in the fridge and use within 7 days.

6. The curd is best served on scones, toast or even baked in the middle of some sweet pastry. I also believe this would make a nice cheesecake filling if made in the right quantity and placed over a buttery biscuit base.

Japanese Knotweed
& Apple Crumble

People are always amazed when I serve them this dessert. The idea that Japanese Knotweed might actually be edible is enough to get questions flying, moreover you can make it taste as nice as this. The next question is "where is it growing around here?". This is a classic dessert given a wild food twist. The stalks have to be young and fresh for this recipe.

Ingredients:

- 2 large cooking apples - peeled, chopped & cored

- 5 stalks Japanese Knotweed - roughly chopped

- 50g caster sugar

- 120g brown sugar

- 60g butter

- 100g flour

- 200ml thick cream or vanilla ice cream

Method:

1. Preheat oven to 200C or gas mark 6.

2. Combine the apple and Japanese Knotweed in an oven-proof dish, then sprinkle over the caster sugar.

3. Add brown sugar, butter and flour to a bowl and mix with your hands until it's nice and crumbly.

4. Spread the crumble mixture over the top of the apple and Japanese Knotweed mix.

5. Bake in preheated oven for 45 minutes or until the top is golden and the fruit mix is bubbling.

6. The recipe is best served with whipped cream or vanilla ice-cream.

SERVES
4-6

Japanese Knotweed Syrup

This has a flavour similar to Rhubarb syrup. It can be used for making Knotweed lollipops, as well as Japanese Knotweed lemonade which is lovely with added lemon and salt. The great thing with this recipe is the fact that it can be done later in the year with the older Knotweed stems which are too fibrous for eating.

MAKES
500ML
SYRUP

Ingredients:

- 300g chopped knotweed stems
- 300ml water
- 300g sugar

Method:

1. Place the stalks and water in a large pan and bring to the boil. With the lid on the pan boil for 10 minutes, or until the stems have turned to a pulp.

2. Set a fine-mesh strainer over a large bowl. Pour the knotweed and water through the sieve and push lightly with a spoon, extracting as much juice as possible.

3. Pour this liquid back into your clean pan and add the sugar. Heat for 10 minutes until all of the sugar is dissolved.

4. Carefully pour the syrup into a clean bottle. If you want it to look pink/red add a little food colouring. You can use the syrup in any recipe that calls for rhubarb... as a cordial, in tea, as part of a cheesecake, to make flavoured toppings and much more!

Japanese/ Dog Rose

'rosa canina/rugosa'

Family:

Rosaceae

Habitat:

Japanese/Dog Rose is found on the coast and inland, in broadleaf woodland, in hedgerows, on the boarders of farmland, over heaths and along country paths.

Physical Characteristics:

This is a deciduous shrub growing from 1-5 metres tall. The plant's numerous stems are woody and strong, containing thorns and prickles all over, which can cause cuts but also allows this plant to climb and hold on to surrounding plants. The leaves grow from 3-6cm long and are odd-pinnate, containing 5-7 leaflets and serrated edges. The top of the leaf is rough and dark green whilst the under-side is slightly lighter with soft hairs all over.
The flowers range from white to pink and light red with yellow stamens, are approximately 3-5cm across and hold 5 petals, typical of flowers in the rose family. The fruit goes from green to a deep orange-red, when ripe. It ranges from a ball or droplet shape as on Japanese rose to more of a rugby ball or egg shape on dog rose.

Distribution:

It is found in Europe, Northern Africa and Western Asia, preferring moist soil.

Known Hazards:

Inside the fruit or the rose hips of this plant, there are seeds that contain many hairs. These are sometimes known as itching powder among children, as it can cause itching of the skin if in contact. Because of this it's important that these hairs are not eaten as irritation of the areas of digestion in the body can occur.

Medicinal Uses:

Dog rose is an astringent, diuretic and laxative. The hips of this rose are recognized for their high amount of vitamin C, being up to 50% more, weight for weight, than oranges. This makes the typical rose hip syrup a suitable additive to rest for cases of colds, influenza and coughs.

Could Be Confused With:

Japanese Rose and Dog Rose can be used simultaneously.

Other Interesting Facts:

Taking the seeds from Dog Rose and placing them either in the pockets or socks of a friend is a brilliant way of getting your own back on them, it acts like a type of itching powder.

Edible Uses:

Leaves: Tea

Flowers: Chopped fresh, syrups, turkish delights, cordials, ice lollies, sorbet, alcohol mixer

Fruit: Syrups, ice cream, juice, soups, fresh (as tomato)

Japanese Rose Hip Ketchup

I had a mad year on ketchups and decided that this rose hip ketchup recipe was my favourite. However, this can also be done with hawthorn berries as well. The ketchup contains all the 5 flavours you expect from a classic sauce and it really delivers. It's an amazing accompaniment to everything you'd use regular ketchup with. I personally like it on venison burgers with dandelion capers, cheese and wild salad.

Ingredients:

- 500g Japanese Rose Hips

- 300ml cider vinegar

- 150g brown sugar or 100ml birch sap syrup

- 1/2 tsp salt or hogweed seed salt

- 1 onion, skinned and finely chopped

Method:

1. Add the rose hips, cider vinegar and water to a large pan and heat, with the lid on for 10 minutes.

2. Pour this in to a blender and blitz until smooth. Then press the whole mixture through a sieve to remove the seeds.

3. In a separate frying pan caramelise the onions with half the sugar.

4. Add the rose hip and cider vinegar juice back to the large pan along with the caramelised onions, the rest of the sugar and the salt. At this point you can make your own additions with chilli flakes, raisins or whatever else you like.

5. Boil vigorously for 10 minutes until thickened.

6. Place in well cleaned jars then use within 1 year and within 2 weeks once opened.

MAKES
3-4
MEDIUM
SIZED
JARS

SERVES
3

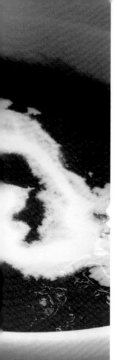

Japanese Rose Hip & Beetroot Soup

This rose hip soup is perfect for the darker days to come and will warm you through. It almost has the flavour of a tomato and beetroot soup and is super high in vitamin C.

Ingredients:

- 2 onions, finely chopped
- 2 whole beetroots, skinned and chopped
- 300g rose hips
- 500ml vegetable stock
- 3 tbsp single cream
- Salt & pepper to season

Method:

1. In a food processor blitz the rose hips with half the vegetable stock, then add to a pan and boil for 10 minutes with the lid on.

2. Pass this mixture through a fine sieve to remove the seeds and add the pulp back to the pan.

3. Add the onions, beetroots and the rest of the vegetable stock and boil for a further 10 minutes.

4. Put the whole lot in a blender and blend until smooth.

5. Serve with a generous dash of salt and pepper and a swirl of single cream in each bowl. This tastes gret with a side of hearty nettle bread.

Japanese Rose Flower Turkish Delights

These Turkish delights really emphasise the fragrant smell and taste of the Rose Flowers. They're sticky, sweet and delicious!

MAKES 30 CUBES

Ingredients:

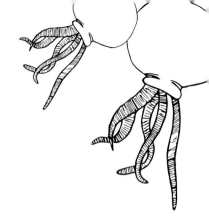

- 8 leaves gelatine (approx 13g)
- 500g caster sugar
- 2 tbsp rose water
- 2 tbsp icing suagr
- 1 tbsp cornflour
- 300ml water

Method:

1. In a large cold pan place the gelatine leaves, break them up if you need to. Cover this with 300ml cold water and leave to soak for 5 minutes.

2. Turn on a low heat and warm the mixture through until the gelatine is fully dissolved in the water. Then add the sugar, keeping the pan on a low heat and stir until it is fully dissolved. Bring to a simmer and leave for 20 minutes.

3. Add the rose water and simmer for a further 2 minutes. Then remove from the heat.

4. Take a small baking tin, 15-20cm square. Any tin will work but this size will give you a more solid final square for your delights. Using your hands rub a little cold water over the whole of the inside of the tin.

5. Pour in your Turkish delight mixture and leave in a cool dry place over night to set properly.

6. The next day, mix the corn flour and icing sugar together in a bowl then sprinkle half of this over a flat surface through a sieve.

7. Remove your set turkish delight mixture on to this side...this can be quite a sticky job. Sprinkle the other half of the icing sugar over the top and cut into squares using a sharp knife.

8. Move these squares around in the icing sugar and cornflour mixture until all sides are covered. Keep your Turkish Delights in a cardboard box with extra icing sugar and eat within 1 week.

Japanese Rose Hip Syrup On Irish Pancakes

This syrup is highly nutritious, extremely high in vitamin C, and also cracking in loads of food situations. I'm using it here on Irish pancakes, but it can also be used for making ice lollies, over deserts, in hot drinks, in ice creams, sorbets, jellies and much more.

Ingredients:

Syrup - 1.5l

- 500g rose hips

- 300g caster sugar

- 1 litre water

Pancakes - for 6 people

- 1 large egg

- 100g self raising flour

- 200ml milk

- 1 tbsp caster sugar

- Butter, for frying

SERVES 6

Method:

1. In a food processor blitz your rose hips, or chop them finely, then add to a pan with ½ the water and boil for 10 minutes with the lid on.

2. Pass through a fine sieve to remove any seeds from the rose hips, then add the rest of the water and mix thoroughly.

3. If you want a fine syrup you can then pass the mixture through a fine muslin cloth, if not follow the next step.

4. Add the sugar and heat the mixture up again, boil for a further 10 minutes.

5. Pour into sterilised or well cleaned jars and use within 1 year, or 2 weeks once opened.

6. In a large bowl place the flour and sugar and combine nicely. Then make a well in the centre and add the milk slowly, combining well as you go.

7. Crack the egg in to the batter mixture and whisk thoroughly.

8. Put the butter in a pan and let it melt. Pour a little of the batter mixture in the pan and fry on both sides for 3 minutes each. Serve up with a dollop of rosehip syrup and enjoy.

Stinging Nettle
'utrica dioica'

Habitat:

Stinging nettles live on roadsides, railway banks, waste ground, hedgerows, urban and sub-urban areas and around field edges.

Distribution:

One of the most prolific plants throughout the UK, Northern Europe, most of Asia, the United States and Canada. Sometimes struggling further South as it prefers moist soil.

Physical Characteristics:

The stinging nettle is a herbaceous perennial, growing back yearly. Typically groups of male and female plants grow separately. It has widely spread rhizomes that are bright yellow along with the roots.

The stem grows from 1-2m tall through the summer and dies down to the ground through the winter. It's hollow, ribbed and houses many fine hairs and stinging needles.

Leaves are pale green, turning darker throughout the year. They have a wide base and a pointed tip with a heavily serrated margin, growing from 3-15cm and are placed oppositely up the stem. It bears very small flowers in densely packed axillary inflorescences.

Known Hazards:

Stinging nettles are well known for the burning sensation they give if handled needlessly. On the stem of a nettle stalk are thousands of small needles, typically pointing upwards, with small sacks at the base of the needle. These sacks are filled with various chemicals some of which are acetylcholine, histamine, 5-HT (serotonin), moroidin, leukotrienes, and possibly formic acid.

Could Be Confused With:

Dead nettles (Lamium Purpureum/Album) look similar and can cause quite a shock when picked with no stings. They don't grow as large as stinging nettles, they don't sting and their flowers grow up the stem looking like small bells. The whole of this plant is also edible and if you suck on the base of the flower you can get a nice hit of sweet juice (must be why the bees seem to like it so much).

Medicinal Uses:

Talking to a range of herbalists, it seems that nettles are the go-to herb for most ailments and they are the lifeblood of current herbalism. Nettle root has been used to help treat prostate cancer and generally helps you keep a healthy prostate. Teas, infusions, creams and tinctures are mainly used to help reduce allergies, stimulate digestion, cleanse blood, aid lactation, reduce inflammation, promote menstruation, relieve pain, kill germs, stop hair loss, lower body temperature, increase urination, stop bleeding, dilate blood vessels, lower blood pressure and to heal wounds.

The use of nettles is proven to aid arthritis, although clinical trials isolated a number of chemicals present in the nettle for tests. Traditionally you would hit the desired area with the stinging nettle for up to 20 minutes, causing the heat sensation for a number of hours.

Edible Uses:

Root: herbal use

Stem: edible when young, becomes fibrous with age.

Leaves young: lacto ferment, spinach sub, crisps, pickled, soups, pesto, sauce

Leaves old: powdered, cordial, syrup, stock

Fruit/seeds: edible, roasted, fried

Other Interesting Facts:

Fibres from the stem of this plant make an extremely strong cord and can be spun very finely to also make thread. Interestingly, a number of companies around the world are looking into this plant for potential use as cloth and clothing.

SERVES 1

Nettle Leaf & Pear Smoothie

I got the idea to make this smoothie after seeing a lot of pear and spinach smoothies around in health food cafés. I thought "well that might be good with nettles instead of spinach" and I was right. This is a hearty smoothie, perfect for enjoying cooled on a summers day or to keep away that mid-morning hunger – either way, it's truly delicious.

Ingredients:

- 1 pear, chopped with the middle removed

- 5 nettle tops, washed

- 200ml hazelnut milk (or regular milk)

- 2 ice cubes

Method:

1. Throw all the ingredients into a blender or smoothie machine and blend until nice and smooth.

2. Enjoy chilled.

3. The recipe also works well as a winter smoothie if you remove the ice and use half a thumb of ginger instead.

This recipe makes enough for around 300ml per person.

Nettle Soup

I've had a lot of bad nettle soups but having finally created this recipe I have no need to try any others as it's really perfect.

Ingredients:

- Half a bag of nettles, washed (around 200g)

- 2 large potatoes, peeled and chopped

- 2 onions, skinned and diced

- 50g wild garlic stalks or 2 garlic cloves

- 4 cornered leek stems, chopped or 2 leeks

- 10 ground elder shoots, chopped or 2 celery sticks

- 1.5l vegetable stock

- 50ml single cream

Method:

1. Boil the potatoes and celery for 10 minutes in the vegetable stock.

2. Fry off the onions, leeks, wild garlic stalks and the nettles for 2 minutes until soft.

3. Mix the potatoes, celery and vegetable stock in with the rest of the ingredients, then put into a blender and blend until smooth.

4. Add a swirl of cream in your serving bowl before eating, along with a pinch of salt and pepper.

5. Enjoy with nettle leaf bread or why not add some fried nettle crisps on top of your soup.

SERVES
4

Nettle Leaf Crisps

From my thorough explorations with wild plants, I've found these crisps will always win people over to the simplicity and great flavours that wild plants can offer. They're quick, easy, crispy and extremely tasty – a real crowd pleaser. Once made if they don't get eaten straight away, they can be put on top of a huge range of dishes like salads, soups, pasta dishes and even over ice cream.

Ingredients:

• Half a bag of nettle tops, around 200g

• 100ml vegetable oil

• Hogweed seed seasoning/salt & pepper

Method:

1. Place 20ml of oil in a pan and heat. Leave 1 leaf in the pan from the beginning to see when it begins to cook and bubble.

2. At this point add more nettle leaves. Each leaf needs room to cook, so if you just chuck them all in the pan they will wilt down and not crisp up. Just place a few in the pan at a time.

3. After 1-2 minutes, or when they start turning slightly golden, turn the leaves over and cook the other side. Once cooked, remove and place on some kitchen towel.

4. Add a little more oil and repeat the process with more fresh nettle tops until they're all done. Season with what you have to hand and enjoy.

Lacto-Fermented Nettle Leaves

Lacto fermenting is the process of salt fermenting. The salt itself draws the liquid from the leaves, killing off harmful bacteria, it then allows lacto-bacilli to grow and multiply which can aid digestion. It tastes incredible and can add amazing flavours to other recipes. It can be used in things such as soups, bread, pasta, sauces and much more. On top of all that it's a cracking way to preserve the fresh nettle tops in an easy to access form.

Ingredients:

- A bag of fresh nettle tops, around 400g

- 40g sea/rock salt, finely ground

Method:

1. Put the fresh nettle tops in a large pan with 2tbsp water, heat with the lid on and let them wilt down. This should take about 5 minutes, stirring every minute.

2. Remove from the heat and roughly chop the nettles with a long handled pair of scissors. Then add the salt and mix in thoroughly.

3. Tightly pack in to your well washed jars, making sure all air bubbles are removed and top up with a little extra water to cover the tops of the nettles, then seal.

4. Store and use within 8 weeks. Once opened keep in the fridge and consume within 2 weeks.

MAKES
2-3
MEDIUM
SIZED
JARS

Nettles Tossed In Wild Garlic Cheese

Served with pork chops and roast potatoes, these brilliant ingredients come together perfectly to give you a hearty meal for those wet and cold spring evenings.

Ingredients:

- 200g wild garlic pesto/ regular pesto

- 200g full fat soft cheese

- 4 good quality pork chops

- 12 medium sized potatoes, peeled & halved

- Half a bag of nettle leaves, around 200g

- A small splash of vegetable oil

Method:

1. Put the vegetable oil in a roasting tray and leave in the oven on 200C whilst you boil the potatoes.

2. Put the potatoes in to salted boiling water and boil for 4 minutes, strain in a colander and toss them around to fluff up the edges.

3. Quickly throw them onto the heated roasting tray and leave them in the oven for 45 minutes, tossing them every 15 minutes.

4. Put the pork chops under a hot grill for 4 minutes on each side.

5. Whilst they're both cooking, put your fresh nettle tops into a pan with 1tsp water and heat with the lid on for 4 minutes, stirring until it's all wilted down.

6. Remove from the heat and strain the mixture in your colander. Place back in the pan with the wild garlic pesto and full fat cheese and heat for a further 2 minutes.

7. Remove the potatoes and pork from the heat and plate up along with the wild garlic cheese nettles and enjoy this hearty meal.

Nettle Leaf Bread

A great way to get nettles into your regular eating habits, these can be made at the start of the week and eaten whenever you'd normally reach for bread. This recipe will make 6 large sandwich rolls of nettle bread.

Ingredients:

- 100g nettle tops, wilted in a pan & finely chopped (or 10g dried nettle leaves powdered)

- 1tsp bread yeast

- 500g strong bread flour

- 1tbsp birch sap syrup or honey

- 2tbsp olive oil

- 350ml water

- 50g salted butter, melted

- 1tsp salt, ground

Method:

1. In a large bowl mix the flour, salt and yeast together dry.

2. Make a well in the centre and add your birch sap syrup, olive oil, water and chopped nettles. Mix thoroughly with a spoon then lay out on a floured surface.

3. Knead the mixture with your hands for 10 minutes – be firm with the kneading, pulling the edges to the centre and pushing down firmly. When it's ready it shouldn't stick to your hands but should be elastic.

4. Place the dough back in your large bowl with some cling film over the top and leave somewhere warm for 2 hours – by this time it should have doubled in size.

5. Cut into 6 equal portions and round each into a ball. Place these onto a greased baking tray and leave for a further 30 minutes to rise again. Once risen, brush the top with the melted butter and place in the oven - 200C for 35 minutes. They will be ready when they sound hollow if you knock on the bottom of them.

Enjoy filled with your favourite sandwich filling, with a bowl of nettle or other soup or with a little of the sweet ciceley and marrow fat bean side dish on.

SERVES
6

Nettle Leaf Pasta

Nettle pasta has an amazing green marbled look and packs all of the health benefits, vitamins, minerals and nutrients that are in fresh Nettle tops. It can add another great wild element to your dish and what better base to have to a dish than fresh Nettle leaf pasta.

**SERVES
1**

Ingredients:

- 100g plain flour
- 1 egg
- 5 nettle tops

Method:

1. Chop the nettle tops and crush in a pestle and mortar, straining away the juice. If you don't have a pestle and mortar, you can just chop the nettle tops very finely.

2. Put the flour in a big bowl, add the nettles and mix, then make a well in the centre. Crack the egg and pour into the well.

3. Mix the whole lot until you end up with a nice dough, it shouldn't stick to your hands, if it does add more flour.

4. Knead the dough vigorously on a hard secure surface for 5-10minutes. It should be elastic and hold its shape well. After this, place the dough in cling film and leave to rest for 1 hour in the fridge.

5. Pass the mixture through your pasta roller or roll out very finely using a rolling pin. Use extra flour to coat the dough and surfaces and then cut into strips. You can cut these however thick you'd like your pasta.

6. Place in boiling water to cook for 2-3 minutes. You can test if the pasta is cooked by removing a little and tasting. It should be elastic and have a little bite.

Enjoy with wild garlic pesto or use in whatever dish you would usually use pasta for.

MAKES
1 LITRE

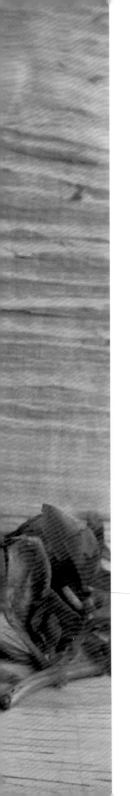

Nettle Leaf Cordial

This surprising use of nettles will leave you amazed and running off to your nearest nettle patch with a set of marigolds pulled up to your elbows. It's a great way to use up the older, more fibrous nettle leaves that you wouldn't eat in other recipes. This recipe makes around 1 litre of cordial.

Ingredients:

- 200g nettle leaves

- 500g caster sugar

- 4 squeezed lemons / 4tbsp lemon juice

- 500ml water

Method:

1. Boil the nettles in the water for around 15 minutes and then strain.

2. To the strained liquid, add the lemon juice and sugar and heat on a low heat until the sugar has dissolved. Then bring up to boiling point.

3. Pour into steralised bottles and enjoy!

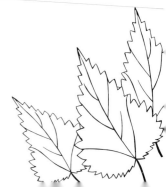

Nettle Pasta Wild Wontons

This recipe is one of my favourites as it's very versatile. As long as you get the base ingredients correct you can add any wild ingredient in to the mix. You can either make your own wonton sheets or buy them online pre-made, it's totally up to you. However I like to use a basic thin nettle pasta sheet as my wonton wrapper.

Ingredients:

Wontons

- Wonton wrapper

- 1 carrot

- 1/2 onion

- 10g wild garlic or 1 garlic bulb

- 1/2 thumb fresh ginger, peeled

- 1/2 veg stock cube

- 100g finely chopped wild ingredients eg: hogweed stems, nettles, dandelion, hazelnuts

- Vegetable oil

Dipping Sauce

- 2 tbsp dandelion flower marmalade

- 2 tbsp soy sauce

Method:

1. Take your carrot, onion, garlic, ginger and stock cube and blitz them finely in a food processor; not to a mush but so it's really finely chopped, or just chop it really finely.

2. To this add your finely chopped wild ingredients and mix together. This is now your filling.

3. Take your wonton wrapper and place a small amount of the filling in the centre. Use your finger and a little water to wet the edges of the wrapper and fold together to seal the edges. Place on a sheet of non-stick paper and continue.

4. Once they're all made, heat up a little oil in a non-stick pan and once hot, place your wontons in. Make sure they're not touching one another and do it in a couple of batches. Fry until golden brown on both sides, remove and place on a piece of kitchen roll to absorb any extra oil.

5. In a bowl mix the soy sauce and dandelion flower marmalade, this is now your sweet dipping sauce. Take a wonton, dip it in some sweet dipping sauce and enjoy!

Wood Sorrel
'oxalis acetosella'

Habitat:

Wood Sorrel which comes from the Oxalidaceae family, grows mainly in damp woodlands.

Distribution:

Wood Sorrel can be found across the UK, most of Europe (specifically Northern Europe), Northern America and most of Asia.

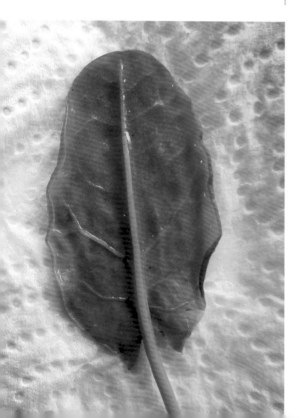

Physical Characteristics:

This common perennial can grow in large patches connected by subterranean rhizomes, with the ability to produce by seed and by rhizome.

There are no stems, rather clumps of leaves growing together from 5-10cm in length. Each leaf collection is made up of three heart shaped leaflets. Each leaf has a fold down its centre which changes, opening and closing dependent on the amount of light available.

This plant amazingly has two types of flower. Its first set of flowers from deep purple to white with distinct purple-white veins, are incredibly attractive, opening up and inviting many bumble bees. The second set of flower that appear later in the year are called cleistogamous flower, these are very small, remaining fully closed and will self-pollinate.

Could Be Confused With:

Wood Sorrels can easily be confused with clover. The leaves are quite similar, with the main difference being that a clover leaf sits flat, whereas a sorrel leaf has a distinct fold down the centre of the leaf, making each leaf almost look like the wings of a butterfly.

Medicinal Uses:

The Wood Sorrel is a diuretic and has antiscorbutic properties as well has having a great cooling ability. It has been used to calm stomach upsets.

Known Hazards:

Wood Sorrel, similar to rhubarb, contains oxalic acid, giving it its sour taste. If you ingest too much of this acid you can upset your stomach. Saying that, you would have to eat a serious amount of Wood Sorrel to get to this point. It is to be avoided by anyone with kidney disease, kidney stones, rheumatoid arthritis, or gout.

Edible Uses:

Leaves: edible salads, sauces, smoothies, juiced, cakes, icing

Flower: all of the above

Sorrel Sauce & Mackerel

Sorrel has a lemony and zesty flavour that lends itself perfectly to fish. You can simply stuff fish with sorrel leaves before cooking, marinade the fish in blitzed sorrel and oil or make this delicious sorrel sauce to accompany cooked fish.

Ingredients:

- 2 mackerel fillets

- 15g sorrel (whole if wood sorrel or roughly chopped if lambs sorrel)

- 5 tbsp double cream

- 1 egg yolk

- 200g new potatoes

- 1 tbsp salted butter

- 1 garlic clove, chopped

Method:

1. Heat a medium pan of water until boiling and then add the whole new potatoes.

2. Boil for 12-15 minutes until tender, then strain and stir in the butter.

3. Heat a large non-stick pan with a little oil. Season the mackerel fillets well and place them in the hot pan, skin side down and cook for 2 minutes until the skin is nice and crisp. Turn them over and cook for a further 30 seconds then remove from the pan onto a plate.

4. In the same pan add the garlic and all the double cream, heat for about 2 minutes.

5. Remove from the heat and beat in the egg yolk until a thick sauce is reached. This should take about 30 seconds.

6. Season the sauce well (preferably with alexanders seeds and sea salt, but salt and pepper will work) and stir in the sorrel leaves and stalks.

7. Plate up the new potatoes and fish and pour the hot sauce over the top.

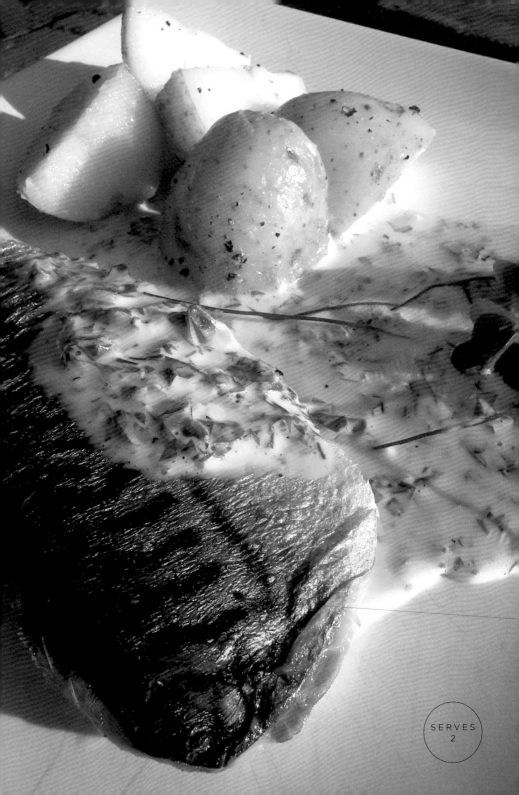

SERVES
2

SERVES
1

Sorrel & Strawberry Smoothie

This smoothie has a reminiscent taste of strawberry lemonade. It's perfect for refreshing your body on what promises to be a warm summers day! I drink this at the start of the day with breakfast to help wake me up, but this could inevitably be enjoyed at any time. The lemon hit you get from sorrel really complements the strawberries.

Ingredients:

- 1/4 tsp salt

- 40ml water

- 30 lambs sorrel leaves or 45 wood sorrel leaves

- 3 cups of strawberries (use the cup you will drink from)

- 1 cup of ice

- 6 tbsp vanilla yoghurt

Method:

1. Throw all the ingredients into a blender and blitz until smooth.

2. You can enjoy the smoothie like this or if you place the mixture into an ice cream churner you can turn it into a frozen yoghurt!

Sorrel & Water Mint Mojito

There are a lot of different wild cocktails you could make...in fact you could write a book on it! However this is one of my favourites! I initially love mojitos and was delighted when I came up with this wild mojito recipe. I've not yet met a single person who hasn't enjoyed it!

Ingredients:

- 2 shots Bacardi or other white rum

- 1 shot birch sap syrup or sugar syrup

- 8 water mint leaves or regular mint leaves

- 15 lambs sorrel leaves or 30 wood sorrel leaves or a wedge of lime

- 100ml soda water

- Crushed ice

Method:

1. Put the birch sap syrup and sorrel leaves into a glass, and with a muddler, squish the sorrel leaves into the syrup for around 30 seconds. You'll more than likely make the leaves into a bit of a mush to release the flavour. If you don't have a muddler, you could use the end of something solid, like a rolling pin.

2. Add the mint leaves and push down another 5 times to open up the flavour in them. Then pour in your white rum and stir.

3. Fill the rest of the glass with crushed ice and pour the soda water to the top of the glass. Now use a long spoon to stir the mixture and infuse the flavours throughout.

4. Serve with a garnish of sorrel leaf and water mint leaf.

SERVES
1

Sweet Cicely

'myrrhis odorata'

Habitat:

Sweet cicely grows around garden edges, sunny spots and hedgerow edges.

Distribution:

Sweet cicely is found in the UK and the most temperate regions of Europe, America and Asia.

Physical Characteristics:

Sweet cicely is a perennial growing to 1 metre high and 1 metre across in full bloom.

It has a rounded hollow stem with down hairs all over, giving it a slight velvety feel.

The flowers are white, but can be slightly pink on occasion. They're based in medium sized long stalked umbels 2-4cm across with 5-12 umbels coming from each plant.

The fruit/seeds are an elongated rugby ball shape from 1-2cm in length, beginning green and turning black as they mature.

The leaves are up to 30cm long and appear fern like and are 1-3 times pinnate.

A thick pale yellow parsnip like root grows to 20cms down.

Could Be Confused With:

Sweet Cicely could be confused with Cows Parsley (Anthriscus ylvestris) very easily. The leaves are almost identical although Sweet Cicely leaves are a little softer to touch. The flower bunches of Sweet Cicely are smaller than those from cows parsley and the seeds are more elongated and will turn black. Hemlock (Conium Maculatum) looks similar in leaf structure and flower, however it grows to a larger size and has purple blotches over its stem which Sweet Cicely does not. The easiest way to tell these two apart is from the smell of aniseed as you break the stem and seed.

Medicinal Uses:

A tonic can be made out of the whole plant that will aid digestion and will promote an appetite. The volatile oils and flavonoid extracted through an alcohol infusion can act as a blood purifier. It's also referenced that an infusion of the roots in tea will give lethargic people a lift of life and boost of confidence.

Other Interesting Facts:

This is the perfect plant for eating whilst on a walk. It gives you the feeling of a sugar boost and the seeds are easy to carry and keep nibbling on.

Although there's a poisoness look-alike to this plant, I always advise beginner foragers to find this plant. The aniseed smell and flavour makes it easily distinguishable from every other plant in the Umbellifer family – apart from fennel of course.

Edible Uses:

Root: Eaten raw thinly sliced in salads and other dishes, boiled similar to parsnips

Stem/leaves: syrup, candied, salads, sliced in all dishes, sparkling wine, lemonade, as a straw

Seeds when green: dried and powdered, as seasoning, as flavor boost, candied

SERVES
4

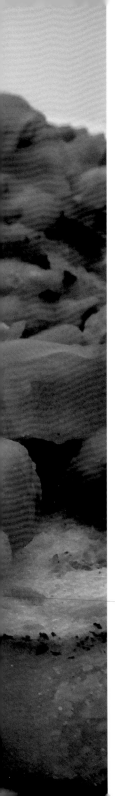

Sweet Cicely, Wild Garlic & Marrow Beans

This side dish is nice to enjoy with a fish dish or served straight on to a nice toasted and oiled piece of ciabatta. You could even just simply toss it through some pasta. There are lots of ways to use this! This recipe will make a bowls worth, which would make a good side for 4 people.

Ingredients:

- 200g diced bacon

- 2 wild garlic stalks chopped, or 2 garlic cloves

- 2 onions, finely chopped

- 500g tin marrowfat peas, drained

- 10g sweet cicely seeds

- 50ml vegetable stock

Method:

1. Place the bacon and onions in a hot pan and cook until golden brown.

2. Add the stock and boil down until the liquid has almost all gone.

3. Add the wild garlic and drained marrowfat peas and cook for a further minute.

4. Remove from the heat and stir in the sweet cicely seeds.

5. Serve cold or hot!

Sweet Cicely, Sardine & Broccoli Nettle Pasta

This delicious pasta recipe combines wild garlic, sorrel leaves and cob nuts and will make enough to serve four people.

Ingredients:

- Fresh nettle pasta for 4 people or 400g dried pasta

- 200g sprouting broccoli, loosely chopped

- 2 onions, chopped

- 12 wild garlic stalks, chopped or 2 garlic cloves

- 10g fresh sweet cicely seeds

- 50g salted sardines in oil, bones removed

- 20g cob nuts, loosely crushed or crushed mixed nuts

- 20 sorrell leaves or the juice of half a lemon

- 4 tbsp olive oil

Method:

1. Bring a frying pan up to heat and cook the onions in a little oil for around 2 minutes until browning. Add the broccoli, wild garlic, and sardines and cook for a further 2 minutes.

2. At the same time add your fresh pasta to a pan of hot salted water and cook for 2/3 minutes until cooked through.

3. Using tongs remove the pasta and add to the frying pan with the other ingredients.

4. Cook for a further 1 minute, adding the olive oil, cob nuts, sorrel leaves and sweet cicely seeds.

5. Serve up on to four plates and enjoy.

SERVES
4

Sweet Cicely & Water Mint Moroccan Lamb Pitta

This recipe will make 6 well stuffed pittas to serve
6 people or 4 really hungry people!

SERVES
6

Ingredients:

Marinade

- 400g lamb chops
- 50g salted butter
- 2 tsp ground cumin, coriander and paprika
- 12 wild garlic stalks or 3 garlic cloves, finely chopped
- 1 tbsp Mugwort leaves or thyme, finely chopped

Pittas

- Marinated lamb
- 20g fresh sweet cicely seeds or fennel seeds
- 1 grated carrot
- 1 small red onion, roughly chopped
- Dandelion leaves, 3 per pitta
- 6 pittas
- Top leaves of 3 water mint plants
- 200g mayonnaise

Method:

1. Melt the butter and mix all the marinade ingredients together. Marinade the lamb in this for at least 1hr. Doing this overnight would be best.

2. Once marinated, BBQ or grill the lamb for 7 minutes on each side.

3. Whilst this is cooking, make your coleslaw. Mix your carrot, onion, sweet cicely seeds and one tablespoon of mayonnaise together in a bowl.

4. For your mint mayo, finely chop the water mint and add it to the remaining mayonnaise.

5. When your lamb is cooked, remove it from the heat and chop in to small cubes, around 2cm square. Cover with tin foil and leave to rest whilst you prepare your pittas.

6. Whilst the lamb is resting, quickly toast the pittas for 30 seconds on each side. Cut them open and stick in your lamb, coleslaw and dandelion leaves. Finish off with a couple of good dollops of your mint mayonnaise and enjoy!

Wild Cherry
'prunus cerasus'

Habitat:

Wild cherries, from the rosaceae family, are usually found around garden edges, hedges, open fields and planted woodland.

Distribution:

Wild cherries grow well in mainland and northern Europe, England, Western Asia and Northern America.

Physical Characteristics:

Wild Cherry is a deciduous tree growing up to 6 meters tall and has a rough, light to mid brown, bark that can appear to give a dull grey glow.

The leaves are elliptic with acute or pointed tips. The leaf edges are slightly serrated containing long petioles (the stem between leaf and branch).

The flowers display the most amazing bloom throughout May, seeming to cover the whole tree whilst the leaves are still in infancy. Individual flowers, 3-4cm wide, produce 5 distinct white/pink petals.

Multiple rounded fruits stem from the same point on each branch and look like stereotypical cherries, hanging down 2-3cm on their individual stalks.

Known Hazards:

Although no specific mention has been seen for this species, it belongs to a genus where most, if not all members of the genus produce hydrogen cyanide, a poison that gives almonds their characteristic flavour. This toxin is found mainly in the leaves and seed and is readily detected by its bitter taste. It is usually present in too small a quantity to do any harm but any very bitter seed or fruit should not be eaten. In small quantities, hydrogen cyanide has been shown to stimulate respiration and improve digestion, it is also claimed to be of benefit in the treatment of cancer. In excess, however, it can cause respiratory failure and even death.

Medicinal Uses:

Sour cherries have fairly high amounts of melatonin, a chemical vital in regulating human sleep cycles. It has therefore been used in the past to aid sleep patterns of individuals.

Could Be Confused With:

Wild cherry trees could easily be confused with other cherry trees as they are able to hybridise very easily and can be used similarly.

Other Interesting Facts:

This tree bares fruit with a single large pip, meaning you can tap the tree, or remove some of the bark until sap starts to leak from the trunk. This sap can be used as a replacement to gum Arabic in making water colour paints. It must be noted that the sap of the cherry tree will shrink a lot more than gum Arabic and this must be taken into account when adding constituent ingredients to your paint mix (less pigment and honey).

Edible Uses:

Flowers/Blossom: Teas, syrups, cakes, decoration, imparts almond flavour

Fruit/seeds: fruit compote, syrup, alcohol infusions, pies, cakes, cookies, muffins

Wild Cherry Blossom Tea

This tea emits an almond like flavour as do the blossoms eaten straight off the tree. I absolutely love tea, you'll rarely find me without a cup! I also love the fact you can pick this blossom straight from the tree and enjoy it in a not only tasty, but magnificently beautiful looking tea. In Japan they make something called Sakurayu, a salt fermented and dried cherry blossom used for making tea on special occasions. However it's a little sour and I prefer it fresh.

Ingredients:

• 5 cherry blossom flowers

• 200ml boiling water

Method:

1. Place your cherry blossom into a mug and pour over the boiling water.

2. Place a small plate over the top of the mug to let the flavours infuse.

3. Steep for around 6 minutes and enjoy hot.

Wild Cherry Whiskey

Some fruits favour gin, others vodka, but cherries definitely favour whiskey. The earthy malty flavours of whiskey, both heighten and are heightened with the addition of cherries, combining to make a smooth liquor that can be enjoyed both straight and in a long drink on those cold winter nights. I often drink this as a night cap after a long day foraging.

Ingredients:

- 400g wild cherries
- 750ml whiskey
- Sugar to taste

Method:

1. Place your cherries in a zip seal bag and put in the freezer over night.

2. Remove the cherries and place in a 1 litre jar. Then pour over the whiskey and leave to rest for at least 3 months.

3. Once you have rested your cherries for your desired time, strain the mixture through a muslin cloth and add sugar to taste.

4. Enjoy straight or in a cherry whiskey smash...2 shots cherry whiskey, 1 good wedge of lime, ice and filled with coke-a-cola...tasty!

Wild Cherry Jam

Cherry jam is a classic way of preserving a glut of wild cherries. It goes well in cakes and on toast, but don't feel limited by sweets. It can also go into savoury dishes instead of sugar. For example I make a great Chinese dipping sauce with cherry jam and soy sauce.

Ingredients:

- 1kg wild cherries

- 2 cooking apples, peeled & sliced

- 1kg jam sugar

- Juice of 1 lemon

- 100ml water

Method:

1. Take three quarters of the cherries and put them in a large pan with 100ml boiling water. Cook with the lid on for 15 minutes until soft.

2. Whilst the cherries are cooking, use a slotted spoon or knife to remove the stones from the left over quarter of cherries.

3. Pass your softened and cooked cherries through a wide sieve to remove the stones.

4. Add the pre-cooked, sieved cherries and the uncooked de-stoned cherries back to the large pan with the peeled and sliced apples, 1kg of jam sugar and lemon juice.

5. Boil all together for 10-15 mins until the jam has reached its setting point. To test this, put a tsp on a small plate, put in the fridge for 2 minutes then remove to see if it has a skin over it. If it does you have the setting point, if not keep cooking and repeat until you do.

6. Place into well cleaned jars and use within 6 months or two weeks once opened.

MAKES
6
JARS

Wild Cherry Pie

Cherries are a delight to eat! However, the ones I tend to find wild are a little bitter for eating fresh, so this pie is a great way of getting them off the tree and onto your table. Frozen cherries also go a little limp, but that's not an issue in this dish so frozen cherries can also be used. You'll find this vibrant, sweet fruit filling waiting to be eaten beneath a crispy and crunchy, golden brown crusting pastry – dive in. This recipe makes one pie, which will serve 6 people. Try to use a pie dish around 20cm squared and 7cm deep.

SERVES
6

Ingredients:

Filling

- 400g cherries, stones removed & halved
- 150g cherry jam or 100g caster sugar
- 25g salted butter
- Vanilla ice cream to serve

Pastry

- 250g salted butter
- 400g plain flour, plus extra for dusting
- 50ml cherry syrup or 50g caster sugar
- 2 egg yolks - keep the egg whites seperate

Method:

1. For the pastry, place your flour in a large bowl, along with the butter cut into small cubes. Mix into the flour until it resembles bread crumbs and is mixed as well as you can get it.

2. Put the egg yolks and cherry syrup (or sugar) into the bowl and mix thoroughly. It's easiest to do this with your hands.

3. Turn the mixture out onto a floured surface and quickly knead for a minute until it's all sufficiently bound together. Then wrap the mixture in cling film and place in the fridge whilst you make the filling.

4. In another bowl mix the cherries, cherry jam and butter.

5. Remove the pastry from the fridge and split into two equal sized pieces. On a well-floured surface roll the two pieces out until they're about the thickness of a £1 coin. Place one of them in a well greased pie dish so that it covers the base and sides.

6. If you have baking beans use those, or alternatively use well washed 1 & 2 penny pieces. Place a piece of baking paper over your first layer of pastry in the baking dish, then put the beans or pennies on top of this and flash bake for 4 minutes in a pre-heated oven at 180C.

7. Remove from the oven, lifting your baking paper to remove the pennies or beans. Fill your flash baked pastry case with the filling, put the last piece of rolled pastry on top and cut away anything that comes over the edge of the dish. Brush the pastry with your left over egg white and bake for 35 minutes.

8. Leave to cook for at least 15 minutes before serving up with a good dollop of vanilla ice cream.

Wild Garlic
'allium ursinum'

Habitat:

Wild Garlic is typically found in broad leaved woodland, enjoying a moist verge, preferring but not solely found on acidic soil. It tends to leaf and flower before the broad leaved trees come in to leaf and gives the whole woodland an amazing smell of garlic.

Distribution:

Wild garlic is found all over Europe, most of Asia and North America.

Physical Characteristics:

Wild garlic is a bulbous, perennial plant, going into leaf from as early as January. Its leaves are spear shaped with a pointed tip, and can range from 5-15cms in length and 3-6cm wide.

Each plant has one single flower head that sits on top of a solitary stem, shooting up from the centre of the connecting leaves and looks like a white pompom sat on top of a pole. The white flower contains 6 petals ranging from 0.5-1cm in diameter.

The root resembles that of a small but elongated clove of garlic.

Known Hazards:

Reports of toxicity if eating sacks full, but such outcomes no doubt apply to many foods eaten in excess.

Could Be Confused With:

The leaves could potentially be confused with both the poisonous leaves of Lilly of the Valley (Convallaria majalis) and Lords and Ladies (Arum maculatum), although neither of these smell of garlic. The biggest risk is to accidentally gather up Lords and Ladies leaves through being inattentive whilst collecting garlic leaves as these often grow together.

Medicinal Uses:

As with regular garlic, wild garlic helps to reduce blood pressure, therefore aiding heart disease and reducing the chances of a stroke. It's also worth adding that wild garlic has antibacterial, antibiotic and antiseptic properties.

Edible Uses:

Roots and bulb:
Best harvested when the plant is not in leaf from June-January. Use the bulb as regular garlic, although be aware that it is somewhat fibrous. The roots can be dried and powdered to be used as a seasoning. The bulbs also pickle well

Stem/leaves - early Spring:
Salad item, cooked as a vegetable, to flavour oil, as a wrap, for pesto, leaf curd

Flower bud - Feb/March:
Tempura (using stem as handle), pickled

Flower - March/April:
Salads, as a garnish

Immature seeds - May/June:
Salads, garnish, pickled

Mature seeds - May/June:
As a condiment or spice, for sprouting

Wild Garlic Chunky Mayonnaise

This chunky wild garlic mayonnaise is brilliant for those nights when you're having a pick'n'mix of foods that are perfect for dipping. It can be made at the start of the week and used in every way you'd use more common mayonnaise, obviously the ratios can be changed to your liking but this is how I like to make it...

Ingredients:

• 4 egg yolks

• 500ml sunflower/ rapeseed oil

• 1 tbsp white wine vinegar

• 50g wild garlic stems & leaves, finely chopped

• 50g pine nuts, roughly chopped

Method:

1. Put the egg yolks in a large bowl, add the white wine vinegar and begin to whisk.

2. Slowly add the oil a little at a time and whisk thoroughly, in between adding a little more. It will begin to emulsify, resembling more regular mayonnaise. This should take around 3 minutes.

3. Stop whisking and use a large spoon to fold in the wild garlic stems and pine nuts.

4. Enjoy in fajita wraps, with chips or even battered hogweed stems (see page 71).

MAKES 600ML

Wild Garlic Vinegar Pickled

This simple vinegar preservation doesn't take away from the perfect wild garlic flavour that we love, and once made, a teaspoon of pickled garlic can be used in almost any dish.

Ingredients:

- Wild garlic

- White wine vinegar

MAKES 1 JAR

Method:

1. Finely chop your wild garlic. If you have a food processor, you can quickly blitz the garlic until finely chopped (you don't want a mush).

2. Take a sterilised or well washed jar and fill it with your chopped wild garlic until it's loosely packed.

3. Pour in the white wine vinegar, stirring the contents to remove any bubbles until the vinegar covers the garlic.

4. Screw on the lid of the jar and use whenever a recipe calls for garlic! The pickle can be kept for up to 1 year.

Wild Garlic &
Soft Cheese Stuffed
Chicken With Salad

There's absolutely endless ways you can
incorporate wild garlic in to everyday
cooking. I love making this one every year,
and come back to it on a regular basis as
it's quick, easy and extremely tasty.

SERVES
4

Ingredients:

- 4 large chicken breasts
- 50g wild garlic stems, leaves, flowers or seed buds - finely chopped
- 200g full fat soft cheese
- 70g bag of wild rocket salad
- 1 tbsp olive oil
- 8 wooden tooth picks
- 8 cherry tomatoes, quartered
- 1 stick celery, diced

Method:

1. Slice the chicken breast from the side inward, but don't go all the way through – you're opening a space in the middle to place your garlic cheese mixture.

2. Thoroughly mix your wild garlic and soft cheese together.

3. Using a spoon push the garlic cheese mixture in to the slit you made in the chicken – you can't really over fill so use all of the cheese between the four breasts.

4. Use 2 tooth picks per stuffed breast to spike and seal the open cut side of the breast – so the cheese doesn't just fall out.

5. Wrap the four breasts loosely in tinfoil, place on a baking tray in the oven 180C for 25 minutes.

6. Whilst this is cooking away, mix the rocket, tomatoes and celery together and divide evenly between 4 plates.

7. Remove your chicken, plate up next to your salad and drizzle a little olive oil over the lot. Enjoy with a dry white wine on a summers evening.

Wild Garlic & Cheese Scones

For me these signal the end of winter and the beginning of spring. They taste truly amazing and I'm now asked to bake these for every spring occasion. What's even better is that they can be baked and frozen for use later in the year. I just take them back out the freezer, give them an extra 10 minutes in the oven and they're good to go.

MAKES
6-8
SCONES

Ingredients:

- 250g plain flour
- 75g unsalted butter, small chunks
- 1 tsp baking powder
- 1 tsp salt
- 50g mature cheese, grated
- 15-20 stalks/70g young wild garlic leaves and stems, finely chopped
- 150ml milk

Method:

1. Place the flour into a large bowl and add the butter. Rub the flour into the butter until it resembles fine breadcrumbs, working as quickly and lightly as you can.

2. Add the salt, baking powder, grated cheese and chopped wild garlic leaves then mix.

3. Make a well in the middle and add the milk, a little at a time. Mix together with your hands or a large spoon.

4. Grab the mixture out and form a ball in your hands. Flatten the dough into a thick round on a floured surface and cut into wedges. It is best to handle the dough as little as possible. Then place on a lined baking tray - you should easily make 6 large scones or 8 regular sized ones.

5. Bake in the middle of the oven at 180C for 15-20 minutes or until risen and lightly browned.

6. Enjoy straight away with a little butter spread on them or with your favourite soup or pasta dish.

Wild Garlic & Hogweed Stem Pesto Tart

This simple flat tart is absolutely gorgeous. It works as a nice starter, or can be used for a meal where everything is placed on the table and you can pick at what you want.

Ingredients:

- 30 young hogweed stems

- 100g finely grated parmesan

- 250g full fat soft cheese

- 100g wild garlic pesto

- 300g ready rolled puff pastry

- Scattering of salted cob nuts

SERVES
6

Method:

1. Mix your wild garlic pesto with the soft cheese thoroughly.

2. Remove the puff pastry from the packet and slice into 6 even squares.

3. Using a sharp knife, score a 1cm border around each square of puff pastry. Evenly spread your soft cheese and garlic pesto mix in to the centre and up to the scored edge of each pastry square.

4. Lay 5 young hogweed stems in each pastry square, then scatter some cob nuts over the top along with your parmesan cheese.

5. Bake in a preheated oven at 200C for 15 minutes or until golden brown. Enjoy with a fresh salad for a healthy vegetarian spring seasonal celebration.

Wild Garlic Pesto Pasta

The pesto I make with wild garlic is thick, chunky and delicious. It can be used in a huge range of recipes, from stuffing chicken breasts, to serving as wild garlic bread and of course the classic pesto and pasta. It's truly versatile and can be stored in zip seal bags and kept in the freezer for whenever you need it. This recipe is quick, easy and has that classic taste that only simple cooking and fresh ingredients give you.

Ingredients:

- A handful fresh wild garlic, stems & leaves

- A handful nettle tops

- 80g cob nuts/mixed nuts, crushed

- 80g parmesan cheese, grated

- 100ml olive oil

- Basil to taste

- 10 sorrel leaves or the juice of half a lemon

- 400g penne pasta

Method:

1. Bring a pan of water to the boil, add a pinch of salt and the dried pasta, this will take about 8 minutes in which time you can make the pesto.

2. Chop the nettles and wild garlic in to small pieces, use gloves so you don't get stung.

3. If you have a food processor, chuck the nettles, wild garlic, cob nuts, sorrel leaves and basil in and blitz very quickly, 10 seconds at a time so it's well mixed but still crunchy. If you don't have a food processor, you can use a pestle & mortar to grind the ingredients instead.

4. In a bowl mix the garlic, nettle and nut paste to the grated cheese and add oil until you reach a consistency you're happy with, season to taste.

5. Drain the pasta, place in a large bowl and toss the pesto through it. Enjoy with garlic bread and an extra sprinkling of parmesan cheese.

You can store the pesto in the fridge for up to 2 weeks, or alternatively bag and freeze, using within 1 year.

Poisonous Plants

The next three entries are here to give you some
information on the potential poisonous look-alikes
mentioned previously in this book.

Here I name the main differences between these plants
and the great edible ones mentioned earlier on.
This is aimed at putting your mind at rest when
you're out foraging your edible bounty.

What I find quite interesting is that there's historical
reference to all of these 'poisonous' plants being eaten.
When processed in the right way it is believed they
can be digested safely. For example with multiple
cold water infusions and straining, then heating and
dehydrating Lords and Ladies roots can be
made edible...you can actually use them to make cookies.

This section is not here to scare you but to
make you more confident that you're
definitely picking the right thing.

Hemlock Water Dropwort

'oenanthe crocata'

Physical Characteristics:

The plant grows from 50cm-2m in height. The stem is grooved, round and hollow, releasing a yellowish sticky sap when broken.

The green leaves, 1-4cm, are deeply lobed, growing in opposing pairs up the stems and ending with one single leaf at the end (looking more like coriander than anything else).

Flowers are white growing in an umbel. The pale cream roots are swollen and grow in clusters (sometimes called dead man's fingers) which exude a yellowish liquid when snapped.

From the umbellifers in this book, it's different from Sweet Cicely as it doesn't smell like aniseed and the leaves of Sweet Cicely are a lot more fern like. The Hogweed leaf structure is a lot different. They have 3-5 extremely deeply lobed sections and are hairy all over as well as growing up to 55cm in length. Both of the mentioned plants commonly grow away from rivers and don't have the clusters of swollen roots that Hemlock Water Dropwort has.
My advice is that if you're near a river and unsure of what the umbellifer is then just don't risk it.

Habitat:

This plant is found in very damp spaces and typically along river banks.

Known Hazards:

Often seen as the most deadly plant in Europe, symptoms include nausea, vomiting, convulsions and can eventually lead to death. Most people who pick this plant believe it to be wild parsnips.

Lords & Ladies

'arum maculatum'

Habitat:

Lords & Ladies are typically found on roadside verges and in woodlands.

Known Hazards:

Lords & Ladies is a toxic plant. It contains calcium oxylate crystals, which causes skin irritation and if eaten can cause inflammation of the throat. If eating continues it can lead to asphyxiation. Although, if processed correctly, these irritants can be removed and both the leaves and root of the plant have been recorded as being eaten historically.

Physical Characteristics:

Lords and Ladies is a majestic looking plant producing the lord looking flower, and then spike of bright orange/red berries...it can't be missed.

The dark green leaves, from 5-30cm, have elongated lobes at their base, and go to a single point, giving them the appearance of spears. Wild Garlic is sometimes confused with it because of the spears and Lambs Sorrel because of the leaves. However, the Lords & Ladies leaves are a lot larger and darker green than Lambs Sorrel.

The flower forms inside a large sheath called a spathe which appears like a lord or ladies collar. Wild Garlic forms lots of flowers on top of a single stem, looking pom pom like, and Lambs Sorrel has a single spike with lots of tiny pink to red flowers.

The fruit forms on top of a single spike and is bright orange/red. Wild garlic's fruit/seeds are green/pale not this vivid colour. Lambs Sorrel produces small light pinkish seeds which in no way look like Lords & Ladies fruit.

Poison Hemlock
conium maculatum'

Habitat:

Poison Hemlock is found in woodlands and woodland edges. It particularly likes dappled shade.

Known Hazards:

Coniine present in this plant causes nausea and leads to paralysis, affecting the nervous system. If un-treated t eventually leads to suffocation as the cause of death.

Physical Characteristics:

Poison Hemlock grows to around 1.5-2m tall with a green, smooth, rounded, hollow stem. This has red or purple spots all over it, specifically on the lower half of the stem and where the stems connect.

The green leaves, up to 50cm long and 40cm wide are overall triangular in shape and are very lacy and fern like, with individual leaves being two to four pinnate.

The flowering umbels are white and up to 10-15cm across. This plant could be confused with Sweet Cicely mentioned in this book. Amongst other things, Sweet Cicely doesn't contain the purple spots of Poison Hemlock and Sweet Cicely distinctly smells and tastes like aniseed which Poison Hemlock also does not.

The Foragers' Cookbook

OTHER TITLES STILL TO COME:

the coastal edition

the urban edition

the mushroom edition